International Standard Book Number 0-87012-505-2
Library of Congress Catalog Card Number 93-091618
Printed in the United States of America
Copyright © 1993 by John Kincaid
Scott Depot, West Virginia 25560
All rights reserved

Printed by McClain Printing Company
Parsons, West Virginia 26287
1993

TO:

    Janie

    Maggie Jo

    John William

    Joseph Russell

    Kimberly Jayne

And the memory of Eddie Brown

Acknowledgments

Without the love and support of my family, especially my wife, Janie, this book would still be on scratch paper. Thanks also goes to Judie Smith who helped with the editing (blame her for any mistakes) and read all the stupid things that didn't get into these pages.

Disclaimer

I cannot vouch for the veracity of any of the stories in this book. They have all been conjured up from my memory. Does anyone really know how much of their memories have been mingled with their dreams?

Additional Copies

Additional copies may be obtained by sending a check for $5.95 plus 6% sales tax and $1.50 postage and handling to:

> Kincaid Kountry Books
> 105 Cherrywood Addition
> Scott Depot, WV 25560

Just ask for *City Boy*.

Table of Contents

Introduction	i
Getting Started	1
The Woman in the Night	2
Granny's House	4
Monkey in the Family Tree	6
Catching the Fever	7
Heart in the Hills	9
Dance of the Neurons	12
Appalachian Culture Shock	13
Asphalt Superman	14
Kissin' Cousin	16
Those Magical Ethereal Invisible Cars	17
Hunting (and Fishing)	18
The Big One	19
Camping Out	20
Up in the Mountains	21
Moonshine Stills	24
Gourmet Grandpa	25
The Day That I Stole Jesus	26
Sunday Songs	28
To Everything There is Season	29
Bread and Butter Pickles	31
Harbingers of Spring	33
Ode to an Apple Tree	35
Fairy Dust Snow	37
Five Foot Eight, One-o-Five	38
Don't Eat the Green Beans	38
Supurrrlube	39
The Old Rocking Chair	40
Ode to Country Music	41
Musical Memories	43
The Night Visitor	46
The Garden	50
Tall Tales and Other True Stories	51
The Butcher and the Hound Dog	52
The Boy Who Never Struck Out	54
Kamikaze Midnight	55
Josiah Came Knockin'	57

Table of Contents

The Mean, Green, Running Machine	58
Laughing in the Face of Death	60
Don't Go Camping Up Camp Branch Hollow	64
Room at the Inn	66
Philosophy and Potpourri	**67**
Kimberly	68
The Lie	69
Ravished	69
A Poem?	70
The Gift	70
Brevity	71
Mountain Math	72
Conceit	73
Heyday Hole	73
Butterfly Biology	74
Cosmic Handcuffs	74
Trophies	75
Danger in the Newsprint	76
The Siege	77
The Hunter and the Prey	77
Psalm 10111	78
The Unbroken Circle	**79**
Universe Central	80
The Highway Home	81
The Mountain King	84
Eddie Brown	87
The End of an Era	89
Serenity	90

Introduction

It was a soft song
    A strong and soft song
        A strong and soft song of the hills....

Mountain Fever

I was born down in the city,
But raised up on the hill
Where I caught that Mountain Fever
And it lingers with me still.
Now, some say they can cure it,
But I don't really care
'Cause I'll always have a relapse
Drinking in that mountain air
When October sun burns brightly,
Indian summer bids adieu,
And mountains cry gold-red tears
As winter sleep comes into view.
Now, folks are "pertnear" right
When they call it "Almost Heaven".
I know what I'm a-talkin' 'bout
'Cause I've lived here since I's 'leven.
I'm a West Virginia poor boy,
All dressed up in three piece suits,
Who can play your sophistication game,
But will ne'er forget his roots.
Yep, a West Virginia mountaineer,
Perhaps not born but bred,
And these hills will not release me
Until the day they find me dead.

Well folks, there it is. The first poem and general theme of this book. You'll find here a collection of short stories, narrative poems, and light verse that loosely chronicle (non-chronologically) the life of a Detroit-city boy who was transplanted in, "raised" in, and fell in love with the mountains of West Virginia in the early '60's. You'll find some "stuff" that's humorous, some that's serious, some nostalgic or downright sappy sentimental, and some a little religious (but not preachy).

You might even find a corny story or two, but I won't apologize for any of it. You see, I have a song to sing about these mountains and I'm obliged to sing all of the verses. And you'd better be careful when you start reading this book. You might just find yourself humming along with me.

If you've read this far and haven't made up your mind yet about this book, then try *Josiah Came a Knocking*, *The Garden*, or *The Old Rocking Chair* before deciding. For those of you who haven't read this far, don't bother.

As we go along (I'm assuming the rest of you are with me), I'll try to explain phrases that you might not understand. For example, "pertnear" means "pretty near". That wasn't much help, was it? Well, "pertnear" in this context means "almost". I'll also warn you if a poem is going to be sentimental. That will allow you sophisticated folks to skip over it unharmed.

Well, are you ready for the next story? Hope so. So, just relax, kick off your shoes (not a prerequisite, but it helps), and turn the page. Go ahead... a little country never hurt anyone. You can read it in the closet, if you like. Now, if you read this next story and don't like it, then I am in trouble and you might as well put this book back on the shelf.

....Played to the tune of innocent dreams

    Young and innocent dreams

        Young and innocent plain-folk dreams

            Harmonizing our song of the hills....

Getting Started

"'Where shall I begin, please your Majesty?,' he asked. 'Begin at the beginning,' the King said, gravely, 'and go till you come to the end: then stop.'"

                          Lewis Carroll
                          Alice in Wonderland

"What we call the beginning is often the end
And to make an end is to make a beginning.
The end is where we start from."

                          T. S. Eliot
                          Gerontion

"Son, if ya don't get started, ya' ain't never gonna get finished."

                          Pappy Kincaid
                          Philosophy of Potato Digging

The Woman in the Night
Fayette County, West Virginia
July, 1961

A purple roadster screamed around the curve and noisily accelerated through the straight stretch in front of our house to challenge the hill that lay ahead.

"That Wilkie Kincaid! He ain't gonna live long enough to pay taxes if he keeps driving like that." Granny paused. Then came the inevitable question as she lowered her eyebrows, "He didn't drive like that when he took ya to those ball games last winter, did he?"

"Nope, he didn't, Granny," I said defending my seventh-grade basketball coach, and my future position on the team.

We sat quietly for awhile on the porch swing. Occasionally, someone would drive by, honk his horn and give a wave, and we'd belatedly wave back. The heat of the day was slowly giving way to the growing night shadows of the mountains. The grass and the trees were beginning to coax the dew from the air. Just then an old Model-T came lumbering down the hill. The driver honked and waved.

"Now, there goes a good driver," Granny proclaimed.

"Who was that, Granny?"

"Myrtle Thompson. Lives down by Oscar Baylor. She's a widow, ya know."

Yeah, she looked like a widow - old, and frail, and shaky. She looked like she'd been a widow for fifty years. Her husband probably died the day she started driving that Model-T. I thought I'd rather take my chances riding with Wilkie, but I didn't tell Granny that.

The night was growing darker and the dew on the grass was magically transforming into sparkles as the lightning bugs came out of hiding. Crickets began their evening serenade and an occasional bat would swoop above the pear tree beside the road. All of this was accompanied by the syncopated gurgle of the nearby creek. Granny began humming *Bringing in the Sheaves*. For the longest time I never knew what that song was about, but it certainly was comforting to hear her sing it.

"Ya gotta be careful with that Wilkie K ...."

Granny's imminent lecture and the peace of the night were

shattered by a high pitched scream of a woman in distress. The crickets went hush.

"What was that?!" I yelped, practically jumping out of the swing. "Someone's in trouble, Granny!"

"No, Johnny. Shush! Listen!" commanded Granny, tilting her head and lifting her hand to me for silence.

We sat there in the quiet of the night in anticipation... and then she screamed again. It was a high, long, wild scream, sounding as if she were right there at the end of the porch. It was the most terrifying scream that a woman could have ever uttered.

"Granny, what *is* that?!" I demanded.

"Panther," Granny said authoritatively.

"Panther? ... but Mrs. Yuravish says they ain't no such thing."

Just then the scream came again through the night and once again it seemed to be right on top of us.

"Yep, Panther all right. Your Mrs. Yuravish might know her grammar, Johnny, but there's a lifetime of wondrous things in these hills that you'll never read about in her books."

I got up and headed for the door.

"Where ya going, Son. Stay out here with me a while and listen to her scream."

"Nope, Granny. I think I'm going in and say my prayers."

Granny's House
(Warning: Sentimental)

Granny's house is still standing
In the curve beside the road,
But Granny doesn't live there
She moved out many years ago.
It wasn't much to look at
With crooked windows, floors, and doors,
But it had a Mozart tin roof
That played symphonies with the storms.
That old house would shake and rattle
From a freight train pulling cars,
But from its Galileo porch swing
We'd watch mountains kiss the stars.

Now, I never thought I'd be here
Looking back on it this way
Recalling near forgotten memories
Of my long dead childhood days.
Every summer we would gather
From Detroit to Tennessee
To see our West Virginia Granny
And make mountain memories.
And when she'd spread the table
I thought it food fit for a king -
Red-eyed gravy, ham and hot rolls
With fresh cukes, and corn, and beans.
Then with the wild blackberries
Picked from strip mines o'er the hill
She'd serve cobbler pie and ice cream
As I'd sit and eat my fill.
Then we didn't have much TV,
So we'd sit and watch the trees.
Now, you may think that's boring,
But it always seemed to please
As we'd sit and talk (or gossip)
Or play croquet in the yard
Or bounce someone's brand new baby

Or eye uncle's grand new car.

But Granny doesn't live there now.
She's got a mansion with the King,
But I bet in all that splendor
She still owns an old porch swing.

Post Script

Granny Goldie had an el-shaped, four-room house with a bedroom and living room along the front. From the living room, a downhill pathway through the second bedroom led to the kitchen. In back of the kitchen, a bath and utility room had been added to the original house. The floors, doors, and windows, indeed, were crooked. But when you're seven or eight, you're not concerned with square corners and plumb walls. The important thing about Granny's house was the porch swing. And the important thing about the porch swing was the lady who sat in it. I remember just before I was married, Goldie said to me, "Little Johnny, don't talk too much about love, just try to live it." That was my Granny. I guess, we all ought to be more like eight-year-olds - its not where you live, but who you are that counts. Of course, I'm probably preaching to the choir. Most of the folks that need to read this left this book at the Introduction. Oh well, on with the story ....

Monkey in the Family Tree
1983

It started out innocent enough. My wife and I (We've skipped ahead about 25 years, but we'll get back to the 60's in a minute.) were helping our daughter with her school social studies project. She was doing research on our family tree and we were spending the day at the West Virginia Archives. And so, it was there among the microfilm, history books, and census records that we uncovered a real skeleton in our family's past. We had a monkey in our family tree. The story goes like this....

Back in 1807 James and Mary Kincaid moved from old Virginia to Greenbrier County, West Virginia. After about five years, they decided to move further west. They followed the course of what is now Route 60 across Big Sewell mountain, along the New River Gorge and settled near what is now Gauley Bridge at the confluence of the New and Gauley Rivers.

They found a large hollow sycamore tree and decided to make that their home. The sycamore was so large that you could turn inside of it holding a fence rail in your hand. They cut a hole in the front side of the tree for a door and a small hole in the rear for ventilation. They made beds and trundle beds from poles. In a year or so, they added a room to the tree out of logs. My great-great-grandfather, Preston Kincaid, was born in that tree. And so, although I do not believe that humans descended from monkeys, I do know that my ancestors lived like them.

Years later, around 1840, the Kincaid clan moved to nearby Loop Creek and settled what are now the towns of Page and Kincaid. Kincaid is where I grew up as a boy. Yep, my last name is Kincaid and my home town is Kincaid. That and fifty cents will get you a can of soda.

The Kincaids were farmers and merchants, civil servants and ministers, miners and builders. They put down deep roots in those mountains. Roots so deep that, even I, with all my "learning" and high tech sophistication have not, thank God, been able to sever them from my soul.

Catching the Fever
1957

My earliest recollections of West Virginia are not about Granny's house, but about the times I spent visiting my Aunt Jo's house. Aunt Jo lived a couple of miles from Granny in a little hollow called Ingraham Branch. Her house was nestled high on a hill overlooking the valley. I was the only grandchild for several years and my parents got into the habit of passing me around to Dad's brothers and sisters. With two aunts and three uncles on his side of the family, I got passed around a lot. I remember spending months at Aunt Jo's in the summer. It was probably just a week or two, but I recall it being months. For a city boy from Detroit, it certainly was a change of scenery.

Three things stand out in my memory about Aunt Jo's place: the air, the newspaper, and the creek. The air was not like anything I had experienced in Detroit. It smelled different. It tasted different. It sounded different. It looked different. I've never been able to nail down exactly how it was different, but there was a quality about it that I've found nowhere else to this day. Was it the early morning fog that sometimes lingered until noon? Was it *that* silence of the mountains punctuated only by the whisper of the creek or an occasional car on the highway? Or was it the smell of the honeysuckle or the pine trees in Jo's yard? I don't know, but the air was definitely different - and better.

The newspaper was different too. Aunt Jo got the Charleston Gazette which was delivered from fifty miles away. I looked forward to the paper each morning because I wanted to keep up with my beloved Detroit Tigers back home. Those were the days of Al Kaline, Harvey Kuenn, and Sunday Charlie Maxwell and I couldn't wait to read about their exploits. And you know what? The box scores were different in this paper. They had a surrealistic air about them. Perhaps it had something to do with the way it was printed, but opening that sports page was almost like opening the Scriptures. I can't explain it (don't really want to).

Of course, Charleston had their own minor league team called the Senators. The paper would print the scores of the Senator's games in the lower right hand corner of the front page. Depending upon the outcome, a smiling or frowning Senator would also be printed. That team was really bad. I rarely saw a smiling Senator.

The best thing about Aunt Jo's, however, was the creek. I could play there all day. What could you do with a creek? Everything - build dams, fight battles, wade through the Amazon, chase monsters, or catch salamanders. All the accessories - water, rocks, pebbles, salamanders, imagination - were free of charge and you didn't need any batteries. Come to think of it, that must have been where I caught my Mountain Fever. I must have brought it back and infected the whole family. Then Dad must have had a relapse because he moved us back to West Virginia. I'm sure that's what must have happened!

Heart in the Hills

As transplanted West Virginians, my parents lived near downtown Detroit when I was young. For a time Granny and Grandpa lived with us on the second floor of our house. However, they moved back to West Virginia in the mid-1950's and my Grandpa died shortly after that from black lung.

We made many visits to Granny's house while living in Detroit. I always knew when we were nearing our destination. The prophets would begin to speak. Not verbally, mind you, but by the written word. Writing Scriptures and mini-sermons on the rock cliffs along the mountain roads was a common practice in those days. And so, when I would see "Prepare to Meet Thy Maker" scrawled on a rock in a hairpin turn, I knew, provided Dad negotiated the turn, it was time for me to "prepare to meet thy Granny".

"Repent!" the rocks cried out,
As they hung o'er our car in the curve,
As we ascended Deepwater Mountain
Seeking out our heart in the hills.
"Repent and be saved!" another rock called
As we rounded a curve in the sky,
Topping Deepwater Mountain
Seeking out our heart in the hills.
"John 3:16" the rock read straight ahead
As we entered the valley below
Wound by the road that followed Loop Creek
That led to our heart in the hills.

A coal miner's son, my father was he
Just a boy as he left the creek for the sea.
He sailed through the War, and the subs, and the storms,
But he left his heart in the hills.
So he tried to escape to the City of Cars.
In the 50's, 'twas the place to be.
Great mechanic was he; he made diesels hum,
But he tuned his heart to the hills.

When recession set in, he worked to find work
Looking for cars in need of revival.
'Though he'd visit car lots with tools in his hand,
Payday came from his heart in the hills.
"Ten miles from Charleston," I'd proclaim
As our wagon sped along in the night.
So familiar, this trip we often would take
To visit our heart in the hills.
But now this final trek lay before us
From Detroit 'cross the plains of Columbus
To Gallipolis, o'er the big Silver Bridge,
Gateway to our heart in the hills

"To Florida we'll go (someday) - set up a shop,
And we'll fix all the cars in the Keys."
Yes, my dad had his dreams in the rest of the world,
But thank God for his heart in the hills.

Post Script

This is a biographical sketch of my Dad and his decision to move back to West Virginia. The way I recall it, we were on our way to Florida and just stopped by Granny's to visit and decided to stay. (If I'm wrong, Mom, don't correct me; it makes a nice story.) Anyway, Dad built a house next to Granny's house and that's where I lived until the day I ran away to get married. But that's another story for another poem. So, here was a ten-year-old boy from the city suddenly transplanted to the hills. Now, I enjoyed visiting the mountains, but I wasn't too sure about living there. As it turned out, it was the best move Dad ever made.

Of course, as those high brow anthropologists would say, I had to be assimilated into the local culture. In other words, I had to get use to some of the local customs. There were, indeed, great sacrifices to be made - no more lunch with Soupy Sales, no Tiger baseball on TV (or the radio!), no three shopping bags of candy at Halloween, no .... Wait a minute! I wasn't sure I want to sacrifice *that* much.

I had always been a straight 'A' student at Amos Elementary in Detroit, so Mom tried to get me into the right frame of mind for school in the country. She assured me that I would not have to go barefoot, wear bibbed overalls, chew tobacco, or talk dumb. She also warned me that some of those country kids might be just as smart as I was (and she was right, even if I did know who discovered Lake Superior). As it turned out, I do like to go barefoot, I do talk dumb when it works to my advantage, and I've forgotten who discovered Lake Superior.

I think a word or two about "dumb" hillbillies is in order. I've found that my Appalachian background has, in some instances, given me a distinct advantage because people tend to underestimate my abilities when they find out I'm from the hills. Nothing pleases a poor country boy more than to outwit his "sophisticated" competition. In fact there's on old joke that goes like this:

Question: What's the only thing that separates West Virginians from complete idiots?

Answer: The Ohio River.

I hope you folks who live in Ohio take that joke in the spirit in which it is given. (Hint: You can take it, change the words a little, and tell it about folks who live in Kentucky - or just about anywhere, for that matter.)

There's something about living in the mountains that gives one a deep seated sense of practical wisdom to go along with all of your "book learnin'". In many cases, it's an unbeatable combination. Oh well, so much for pontificating ....

Dance of the Neurons

More and more as I grow older

And the neurons begin their dance,

Half-forgotten memories,

Mingled, merged with long-abandoned dreams,

Mutated by heart's desires,

Percolate through the surface of midday thoughts

Before fleeing again amid the neurons.

Memories of times past, gone, forgotten,

Reinvented,

Savored for an instant -

Cherished not for their veracity,

But for their sweet mutability

Appalachian Culture Shock

"I have been a stranger in a strange land."

Exodus 18:3

"Whenever I hear the word 'culture'...I release the safety-catch from my pistol."

Hanns Johst

"For heaven's sake, Johnny, say *ya'll* not *youse guys*."

Jeanette Kincaid,
My mother, circa 1959

Asphalt Superman
Fall 1959

I didn't have any trouble making friends at my new home, but I did have trouble finding them. Two of my road running mates were Manuel and Pee Wee. Manuel was my immediate "next door" neighbor who lived about a quarter of a mile down the road from me. Pee Wee lived another quarter mile down the road from Manuel. The three of us took to running the road, creek, and woods together.

Now, Pee Wee was taller than me and his shoulders were broader than mine. He was fair-haired and fair-skinned and the girls swooned when he passed by. His nickname certainly did not match his physique, but I never questioned how he had acquired such a moniker. It just didn't matter. Manuel, my other side-kick, was poor and black. Now, I tell you that only to make this point: Manuel's skin color was no more important to me than Pee Wee's inappropriate nickname. The three of us liked riding our bikes, fishing, and roaming the woods. That's all that really mattered to an eleven-year-old boy.

In my way of thinking, country roads were much safer than the busy streets of Detroit. After all, at age seven, I was experienced at going four blocks to the Saturday matinee by myself to watch Godzilla destroy Tokyo or the Creature from the Black Lagoon chase girls through the swamp. Coming home was a little tougher because I always anticipated running into the monster of the month in an alleyway. Four lane streets posed no problems, therefore, country roads should be even safer.

As a matter of fact, the only time I was ever chased by a cow was on the streets of Detroit. It is, perhaps, the earliest and vaguest of my memories. We were living across the street from Clark Park, a large park near downtown. One day a truck loaded with cattle wrecked and all of the cattle escaped into the park. They were, quite naturally, frightened and running wild through the streets and park. I recall being on the sidewalk and getting chased onto a neighbor's porch by a monstrous, snorting Godzilla-like animal. Fortunately, Dad leaped across from our porch to ward off the attacker and save me. Unskilled in the art of herding cattle, the police came and shot the wayward bovines. So, you see how dangerous those city streets were. You had to be on the lookout for cars, trucks, Godzilla, and Elsie.

I would soon discover that a country road can be just as deadly as Woodward Ave. at 5:00 PM. Manuel, Pee Wee, and I were down by the creek one day near Manuel's house. We were eating, to the best of my recollection, something called "fox grapes". (Only the Lord knows what they really were.) As we were walking back up the hill from the creek, my world evaporated away. There was no dizziness, no world spinning 'round, no nausea. My world simply - evaporated away. I was no longer there on the hillside. Manuel and Pee Wee were nowhere to be found. I was floating. I was flying like Superman with no earth below me and no stars above me. I was .... regaining consciousness in a hospital emergency room twenty-five miles away.

What had happened was this. We had climbed back up the hill and hopped on our bikes. As we were crossing the road, an "invisible" car rounded the curve and hit me broadside. I took flight over the car, landed on the trunk, and rolled to the pavement. For the life of me, I cannot remember any of this happening. From ten minutes before until at least an hour after the accident, I remember nothing. Absolutely nothing. I imagine, in some way, death will be like that. My earthly world will just evaporate away. So, while I am afraid of dying, I ain't afraid of death.

Except for a bad concussion and a couple of deep cuts on one arm, I was unhurt. No broken bones, no mangled body parts. And there were some definite advantages. I got a new bike. I got out of school for two weeks and my kissing cousin came to visit me everyday. And I learned an important lesson: watch out for those invisible country cars.

Kissin' Cousin

I had a kissin' cousin,
Lived up the road a ways,
Who'd wear next to nothin'
On those long hot summer days.
We'd sit and sip on ice tea
Philosophizing hours by.
At night she'd snuggle with me
Watching Telstar in the sky.
She loved me like no other
She spoke as best of friend,
But sometimes like a mother
Scold me for trouble I was in.
Never knew what was in store
When I'd see that sassy miss,
Like learning wrestling in the floor
Or how to execute a kiss.
But the years grew us apart;
Don't see her anymore.
But sometimes it warms my heart
To think of kissin' cousin just once more.

Post Script

    Having kissin' cousins living nearby was one advantage the mountains had over the city. Now, you could date or marry your kissing cousin, but you'd better not because there would be enough relatives on either side of the family who'd believe that you or your cousin was coming from the wrong side of the family. You'd best not stir up that pot. So, you knew your limits, but that was OK. Sometimes knowing your limits gives you a great deal of freedom.
    I had two kissin' cousins named Patricia and Bobbie Kay. They were, perhaps, the best friends a guy could have when he was growing up. Bobbie Kay was Pee Wee's girl friend, but she would sneak me up on her porch from time to time and teach me the kissing techniques that Pee Wee was teaching her (but we knew our limits, now). Patricia was my mentor.

We could, and did, talk about almost anything freely and didn't have to worry about this boy-girl rejection thing. We, too, would kiss on occasions, but it was purely for the purpose of exchanging information. Yep, sometimes knowing your limitations gives you a great deal of freedom.

Those Magical Ethereal Invisible Cars

Those invisible cars are hard to see,
Except at night when it's hard to see.
Just turn off the lights and there they are!
Those magical, ethereal, invisible cars.
Going sixty miles into a curve
You don't want to sway; don't want to swerve,
So turn off the lights to see where they are!
Those magical, ethereal, invisible cars.
Going eighty miles into a curve
On that side of the road takes lots-a nerve.
You wanna look good before you go far
For those magical, ethereal, invisible cars.
Don't try this by day in the light of the sun
'Cause headlong you'll crash; that ain't any fun.
But at night they are seen as plain as the stars
Those magical, ethereal, invisible cars.

Hunting

Despite my love for the mountains, I was never quite able to get into this hunting thing. My brother, by contrast, seldom fails to bag his limit. Oh, I tried hunting a couple of times, but the only thing I ever shot was a five foot snake that was staring down my neck. And he had to crawl up in the barrel before I could get a good bead on him. Hunting? Tell me, who really wants to eat squirrel brains?

If all you do is "hunting",
You don't really need a gun,
But for some I am a-fearing
It's the killing that's the fun.
If it moves or if it wiggles,
Just fill it full of holes.
We'll worry 'bout it later,
If we blew off someone's nose.
Instead of "hunting", call it "finding".
Now, that's folks proper aim
Like my brother, who is a "finder"
'Cause he always gets his game.
But to me this "hunting" business
Is a royal pain and bore.
Why, if you want some good red meat,
You can buy it at the store.

(and Fishing)

Now when it comes to "fishing"
Folks really named that right
'Cause if they called it "catching",
I'd be fishing through the night.

My Dad is a true hunter. He's been hunting for sixty years and all he's ever killed is time.

The Big One

Survey the rocks.
You must survey the rocks.
Big rocks, smooth rocks, jagged rocks ...
You'd think they'd all be the same by now.
Hasn't there been enough eons
For Mother Earth to wash away all individuality,
To grind them into sameness ...
Neat, orderly, predictable,
Well mannered little children?
Shouldn't they all be the same?
But they're not. So you survey the rocks.
That's what the big one does ...
From the other side.
Survey the water
Slipping through your surveyed rocks;
Transforming into deep pools.
Catch the current.
Follow it down to deep secret places
Under your surveyed rocks.
That's what the big one does ...
From the other side.
Survey the hook,
Mini harpoon, primed for the kill.
Survey the line, invisible strong
That must transcend the two worlds.
Survey the bait. You *must* survey the bait.
Live bait, see-through minnows,
Dead bait, artificial bait
You must survey your bait.
That's what the big one does ...
From the other side.
Cast your chances upon the water,
Hoping you've surveyed just right.
But that's what the big one has done ...
From the other side.
And he never takes chances like you.
Oh, well ....
Maybe next time.

Camping Out

My wettest times, without a doubt,
Were the times when I'd go camping out.
The tent would play a sweet refrain
To the pitter-pat of pouring rain ....

Huddled inside our man-made cocoon,
Ground hard, we struggled to sleep,
But just when I'd get down to snoring,
Through the waterproof tent it would leak.
Water dripped on my nose, or my backside,
Or sometimes straight down in my ear.
So, I'd scurry around for some high ground.
"Is there a dry spot here, anywhere?"

For breakfast: smoked runny egg yoke
With sausage that still looked alive,
And fresh fried hash brown potatoes
With a dash of pine needle "chive".
Gravy that looked like brown jello,
Coffee with asphalt tar taste.
But tears welled my eyes, viewing the dawn
'Cause the fire blew smoke in my face.

By evening your head started itching
And your teeth felt gritty like sand.
And it's hard, after hours of fishing,
To wash minnow smells offa your hands.
We'd sit in firelight; sing camp songs.
So contented. (At least I'd pretend.)
As the storm clouds rolled 'cross the valley
We got ready for "sleeping" again.

Yes, my camping adventures have been
Too profound for mere mortal words.
In truth, I love Mother Nature,
But camping with Her's for her birds.

Up in the Mountains
Fall 1962

Aunt Lucille was a deer widow. Yep, I spelled that right, d-e-e-r. Every summer Uncle Lawrence would come in from Detroit for a couple of weeks of fishing and every fall he would return for the deer season. Lucille would stay at Granny's during his hunting forays. As pretty as she was, I never understood why Uncle Lawrence would want to run off and leave her for so long. Anyway, Granny was proud of her. Lucille's high school graduation picture hung prominently in the living room. She was the only one of Granny's six children who graduated from high school.

Uncle Lawrence always drove a new Buick convertible equipped with all of the best and latest accessories. He also seemed to be the first one in the family to buy any new gadget on the market. This particular year, he brought a movie camera with him and we all gathered in the yard for a photo session. Everyone felt and acted awkwardly as the recording eye was pointed their way. After all, what can you do on the spur of the moment that is worthy of being preserved for posterity? Fortunately, the autumn colors that year were the brightest I have ever seen. The air was the clearest, the leaves were their fullest, and the view of the mountain across the creek from Granny's porch rivaled anything anyone had seen in years. So, Lawrence turned his camera from us awkward humans and panned the beauty of Mother Nature's handiwork. This scene was, indeed, worthy of preserving, and She was not the least embarrassed strutting her stuff.

Uncle Lawrence was soon on his way to a little place called Frost to set up the hunting camp for deer season. Now, there was one thing I had a hard time understanding. The men always talked about going "up in the mountains" to hunt deer. I always thought, "Up in the mountains? What do they mean? You can't get anymore 'up in the mountains' than right here on Loop Creek. Why, all you have to do is get your gun and walk up on the hillside and there you are - 'up in the mountains'." But the men insisted on traveling a hundred miles and living in a tent to get "up in the mountains" for deer season.

Dad and I had been invited to go along, so we left the following night to join the hunting party. We arrived around midnight to a large warm tent, a pile of straw, and sleeping bags. The next morning's dawn revealed what the men meant by "up in the mountains". The mountains were higher and "stronger" here, the air clearer, the trees brighter, the people fewer. We really were "up in the mountains" now. I also understood why the place was called Frost. It was colder than bejeevers outside!

"You guys go hunt," I thought, "I'll stay here and keep the fire going."

We got up early (real early) to prepare for the hunt. That's another thing I had problems with. "Aren't the deer always in the woods? Won't they be there at 10:00 AM just as much as 5:00 AM," I thought. The answer I got when I asked about this only puzzled me more.

"You get up early," Dad explained, "So you can get into the woods and shoot your deer before the other hunters scare them off *up in the mountains*." There was that phrase again.

"Good heavens," I thought, "We are 'up in the mountains'. Hadn't we just driven a hundred miles to get 'up in the mountains'? And, if we aren't 'up in the mountains', why don't we skedattle on up there now (Wherever it is). That way, we can sleep 'till 10 and then get up and wait for the other hunters to drive the deer 'up in the mountains' where we are." As Star Trek's Mr. Spock would say years later, "This 'up in the mountains' stuff isn't logical."

Despite my thoroughly logical proposal, the tradition stood. You had to get up at 5:00 AM, preferably earlier, if you wanted any chance at bagging your deer. Then came the next hurtle - breakfast. There was only one criteria for calling something food in deer camp. It had to be dead. It didn't have to be cooked, it just had to be dead.

"Want some eggs, son?"

"Sure."

The cook, I think it was Lawrence's brother Leroy, swirled an egg in the skillet and poured it into my plate. It was cold. It was dead. It was half cooked. I couldn't eat it. I hate to see animals sacrificed needlessly, don't you?

"Can you cook this a little more?" I asked.

"Ain't got time, son. Got to get outta here and get *up in the mountains* to get yer deer, ya know."

"Don't fight it," I thought, "Just look around for some peanut butter cookies and let's get our butts *up in the mountains* so we can freeze 'em off."

Except for freezing and starving and walking my feet off, I really enjoyed my hunting expeditions... honest, I did. Well, at least I like to think I did. There's nothing like being *up in the mountains* that makes you glad to get back to Loop Creek and civilization. At least, Granny and Lucille could fix a good mess of green beans.

By the way, by the time we had returned, Lucille had gotten the film developed. We all gathered around the screen to view the panoramic view of the autumn hills of Loop Creek. What we saw was a blur of red, and gold, and brown. Lawrence, in his inexperience with his new toy, had panned the hills much too quickly. I guess, sometimes, memories are better than pictures.

Vocabulary Words

bejeevers -   An untranslatable expression denoting an extreme condition, as in "colder than bejeevers".

skedattle -   To go quickly or in haste, as in "skedattle out of here".

Moonshine Stills

People who don't live in the mountains have accumulated a lot of misconceptions about moonshine and moonshiners. A lot of half-truths and innuendoes have been floating around this country for years. Well, as a teenager growing up in the mountains, I was afforded the opportunity to see moonshining first hand. So, I've written this poem in hopes of shedding some light on one of America's much maligned subcultures.

You may be disappointed
In my tale 'bout moonshine stills
'Caused I ain't never see one
'Though I've lived here all these years.
Why, I've lived up in these hollers
Pertnear all my life
And never seen a moonshine still.
You can go and ask my wife.
White Lightning stills don't exist.
They're just mountain mythology
Perpetuated by us local folk
To keep the truth from you, you see.
So I'll tell you what my Pappy'd say
When the Feds come snooping round.
"We don't brew this stuff in a still;
We pump it from the ground!
Like methane gas and crude oil
It's a natural resource,
So we don't need no moonshine still"....
(But there's a "pump" under the porch.)

Post Script

Well, now you know it. The truth is out. Actually, I never have seen a still and Pappy never had a "pump" under the porch, but he did brew beer under the kitchen. I have tasted White Lightning; it beats the taste of grits, hands down. By the way, "holler" means "hollow, a small steep valley".

Gourmet Grandpa

When Grandpa had a hungering
And nothin' seemed to hit the spot,
He'd grab a bag of pinto beans
And boil 'em in a pot.
Then he'd add some fatback bacon
'Cause you always need your fat!
And no whimpy dieticain
Could talk Grandpa out of that.
Then a bunch of chili peppers
He'd throw into his brew.
For a measure of good seasonin',
Add a garlic bulb or two.
The hotter, man, the better,
Throw some scallions in a bowl.
Top it off with red-hot chow chow
And your eyes began to roll.
It would burn right past your tonsils.
It would almost melt your teeth
And two or three days later
Of garlic you would reek.
But Grandpa liked it that way;
'Twas no food for the meek,
'Cause when he brewed a real good patch,
It'd make you sick for half a week.

Post Script

    The Grandpa in this story was actually my wife's Grandpa, who lived with us a few years before he died in the mid-1970's. He did a lot of cooking. (I found out exactly how much after he died and my wife had to start cooking again.) Grandpa Bill Potter was on a high fat, high salt, high cholesterol, high sugar diet. He smoked and chewed, drank some, and even caroused around a little. It ruined his health. He died premature at 82. I'll pass on to you, free of charge, his advice about marriage: "The man is the head of the house, but it's the woman who turns the neck." That may not be original advice and it may be a little old fashioned, but it's a system that works well.

The Day That I Stole Jesus
1959

This isn't a tale of treachery and murder, but it is a tale of thievery and cowardice. Although my parents were fifth generation West Virginians, we lived in Detroit in my earliest years. I was, perhaps, only in the second or third grade when I embarked upon my life of crime. Although I did earn some honest money by shoveling snow from sidewalks, most of my money-making schemes were either royal flimflams or outright thievery.

One of my scams worked only around Christmas and it required a small investment. I would go down to the corner grocery and buy a bag of potato chips and proceed outside to the trees on display. Sitting under a pine tree and munching quietly on those chips worked magic on passers-by. Many of them actually stopped and gave me money! Of course, the little cup by my side helped things along. This scam was particularly helpful when it was snowing. To this day, almost nothing beats the smell of snow, pine trees, and potato chips.

Another scam of mine involved getting dressed in my Cub Scout suit and soliciting door-to-door for coat hangers. "We're collecting them for a project," I'd tell people. Lie! I'd take my ill begotten hangers down to the dry cleaners and sell them two for a penny. (Did you know that the smell of a dry cleaners hasn't changed in thirty-five years. Every time I pass by one I have flashbacks of my time of crime.) When it came to coat hangers, the city offered unlimited potential. You could go a block or two in any direction and nobody knew you. The lie, that secret sin, was well covered.

My scheming took on new dimensions when I began to steal pop bottles from back porches for the deposit money. I remember one time (Sorry, Mom, it's true.) when I climbed a fence at the corner grocery and stole bottles in order to cash them in the next day. I was headed for destruction.

Fortunately, my parents unwittingly cut short my crime spree, at least temporarily, when they moved us back to West Virginia. We moved next door to my Gramma. There were no more than two dozen houses within a mile radius and the nearest dry cleaners was ten miles away. My revenue sources dried up quickly. I managed to survive for a while. And then it happened. I stole Jesus.

Well, I didn't really steal Jesus. I stole Gramma's picture of Him. I don't recall exactly how it came into my possession. I'm sure that I didn't take it off the wall. It must have been lying around somewhere and I just picked it up.

"She doesn't need it," I thought. "She'll never miss it."

And so, I attempted to peddle it in the neighborhood, but soon discovered that no one was either rich or religious enough to buy it. So I hid it under a rock on the hill in the curve next to our house to wait for another day to make my sell.

Well, Gramma did miss the picture and I became a prime suspect. But I was able to fib my way out of it and managed not to inadvertently confess. I had every intention after that to retrieve and return the picture. But I had to go to school the next day, and I had to do something else the next, and I forgot the next, ... and by the time I uncovered the picture from the rock it had irretrievably succumbed to the elements. It could not be returned. I was too much of a coward to tell Granny what had happened, so I buried that lie, that secret sin, with the rest.

A couple of years later, however, Jesus took "revenge" on me for what I had done to His picture. One night in the autumn chill in the Page Baptist Church, I confessed my secret sins to Him. Sins which He already knew. On that night, He "kidnapped" my heart and soul with love. It's been thirty years now. He hasn't released them yet. I don't think He ever will. I guess that makes us even.

Sunday Songs

In that old country church
We'd sing the old songs,
And yearn for the new song in heaven.
Where the old's passed away
And the Ancient of Days
Reigns supreme from His throne room in heaven.
Those old gospel songs,
So pure and so strong,
Would transport our souls up to heaven.
Where the moon, and the stars,
And the earth fled away,
As we peeked through the veil into heaven.
And we wept as we sang
The mysteries of God
Drawing hearts upward t'ward heaven.
From this prison of clay
They'd sweep us away
To give us a glimpse of God's heaven.
For that *Blessed Assurance*,
Amazing Grace,
We'd lift up our praises to heaven.
While we're *Traveling On*,
It is Well With Our Souls,
But we long for the roll call in heaven.

To Everything There is a Season
1963

It was an extremely hot day in May as we gathered in the small rundown church on the hill near the school. The sun was shining brightly as the wind slept among the newborn leaves and flowers. The congregation slid quietly and respectfully into their seats as the minister prepared for the service. The windows had been opened in a futile attempt to cool the sweltering sanctuary. But the wind continued to sleep. I took my position near the front as the women sat fanning themselves with small paper folding fans. All of the fans were alike. On one side was a picture of Jesus at the Last Supper. On the other side was an advertisement for the local funeral home - "Your Friend in Time of Need". As the inevitable beginning of the service approached, several of the women began to sigh and sob - softly at first, but ever louder as the service began. Try as they might, they could not fan away the heat, nor the grief, that had overcome them.

I sat there near the front pew watching my friend Richard who had been unaffected by all the goings-on. He was untouched by the swelter, and the sighs, and the sobs, and the grief. As I watched him, two well dress men approached the casket, moved some flowers, and deftly closed and locked the lid. Richard was gone.

As the service started, I began thinking of my friend who had been the star of the eighth-grade basketball team. At six-foot-one or so, he played center. Wilkie and Doug, the two young college kids who served as our coaches, had taught him all the moves. In my youthful estimation he moved like a giant on the court, dominating the opposition. Just a few months earlier he had led us to victory in the local eighth-grade tournament. We were Champs and we reveled as teammates. I remember envying him in practice because I was only second string. I remember us singing *The Duke of Earl* in the back seat of Wilkie's roadster as we wound through the New River gorge after a rousing victory at Lookout. I had even scored twelve points that night! I remember us breaking into the school gym to play on Saturday mornings. And I remember the curve in which he died. I have never driven through that curve without thinking of Richard, if but for a brief, fleeting second. He was my teammate. He was my friend.

Someone began to sing, "*Precious Memories, how they linger, how they ever flood my soul.*" The sobs from the women became uncontrollable at that point and their grief overflowed onto us all. I learned that day it's OK to cry when you have something to cry about.

At the end of the service, I rose with my teammates and coaches as we carried Richard to the hearse and out of my fading memories to sleep with the wind among the flowers.

I was puzzled, at the time, why none of the teachers attended Richard's funeral. With many of his classmates there, the teachers' absence was conspicuous - especially in such a small community. But time and experience have suggested an answer: Richard was black. God forgive them for the season in which they lived.

Bread and Butter Pickles

Between Granny's house and our house stood the cellar. It was actually a combination cellar and apartment. The lower level was built into the hillside and housed a small sink, stove, and shelves for canned goods. It had a small window in the front and one on the side just above the stove. Atop the cellar was a small two-room "anything", accessed by climbing the hill that sloped up from the entrance door to the cellar. I call it a two-room "anything" because over the years it was used for almost anything. Uncle Jeep and his new bride lived there for a year or two until I scared him off with a dead rattlesnake. I used it as an apartment while I attended college. Dad used it for a potato bin. Granny used it for storing "junk" and my brother used it to hide his Playboys.

In the corner of the cellar lay the electric water pump, a relatively new addition to the plumbing system at Kincaid Acres. All of our water was supplied by a hand dug well in front of the cellar. The old hand pump still stood atop the well. I remember many a summer's day when we'd pump and pump the rickety old handle. You could hear the water churning as it rose higher and higher in the pipe until it sprang forth, cold and sweet, from the spigot. But the old hand pump stood abandoned most of the time, having been replaced by its newfangled electric cousin.

The World Series was played right there in the yard in front of that cellar, right next to the water pump. That's right, the World Series. All you had to do was take a piece of chalk, draw a strike zone on the cinder blocks, grab a glove and a rubber ball, and you were in business. Just imagine - bases loaded, one run lead, three balls, two strikes, two out, bottom of the ninth. It was just me and my fastball against Mickey Mantle, the home run king. Glory was mine for the strikeout. Checking the runners, I'd settle my nerves and concentrate on the do-or-die pitch. Deftly, I'd complete my windup and the ball would explode from my hand, hurtling toward the plate. Mickey would swing. The crowd would jump to its feet, roaring with excitement. Of course, you know how it ends. After all, it was my World Series.

After the World Series I'd go in and check on the canning. The cellar was a flurry of activity in late summer and early fall. At that time of year Mom and Granny fell into some kind of trance and began canning, jelling, and pickling anything in sight. I swear, if you threw a quart of grub worms their way, they probably would have pickled it. Canned corn, beans, beets, peas, and tomatoes lined the cellar shelves. Added to that were apple jelly, blackberry jelly and jam, rhubarb jam, plum jelly, apple butter, and pear preserves. And then, just before the trance wore off, came the pickling. Sweet pickles, chow chow, pickled beets, pickled corn, picked beans (yes, pickled beans), sauerkraut, and pickled grub worms (see, I told you so) were added to the cellar storehouse.

Mom and Granny, however, were never successful with their dill pickle recipe. Their dill pickles always turned out to be "jolt" pickles - pure salt and vinegar with just the faintest hint of dill. In a perverted way, they were a lot of fun to eat, if you had an iron stomach.

Their best concoction, however, without a doubt, was their Bread and Butter pickles. No grand feast was really complete without them. Thick and sweet and "buttery", those pickles were the best that ever have been made, especially when you found a little clove bud that you could suck on for awhile after the pickle was gone.

Each jar was carefully labeled and dated before it was placed on the shelf. Popular items like Bread and Butter pickles or apple butter went fast. Other things like pickled beets tended to linger in the cellar a little bit longer. In fact, I think that jar of pickled grub worms had been in there since 1926.

Harbingers of Summer
Early 1960's

The true harbingers of summer at Kincaid were the frogs. When the air was filled with uncontrollable croaking and every pond and puddle was full of frogs or black slimy eggs, you knew spring was in full swing and summer was hot on its heels. The frog population in those days was phenomenal. Each spring was almost a reenactment of one of the plagues of Egypt, invoked by Moses and ordained by God. Early on the croaking started and frog upon frog could be seen in any pond. At night the croaking intensified, drowning all of the other night sounds. Later, the ponds would be filled with eggs floating amidst green pond scum. Every few days you could watch the progression as the eggs hatched into young tadpoles or polliwogs, as some would say. As you kept your vigil, the tadpoles would marvelously grow legs and lose their tails as they transformed into frogs - frogs now ready to repeat the cycle. And then, they all disappeared. At least they weren't as visible during the hot summer as they were during breeding season. Where they all went was a mystery, but, like clockwork, they'd be back the next spring.

I must admit that, as a boy, I treated those frogs rather badly. All of the boys would make great sport of throwing rocks at them. We especially liked to throw big rocks that would smash them flat. When someone would get in a really good hit, we'd "ooh", and "aah", and slap each other on the back. Folks get the same kind of thrill today at a football game or when Gallagher, the comic, smashes a big watermelon with his oversized sledgehammer. Now, I'm not telling you what I did was OK. I'm just telling you that I had fun doing it. Besides, what's the difference between getting smashed by a rock and eaten by a snake? And there were plenty of frogs left over, weren't there? Of course, we didn't think twice about impaling a night-crawler or grub worm on a fishing hook, or abusing June bugs. June bugs are relatively large beetles that appear in June (that's why they're called June bugs). They make an interesting buzzing noise when flying around. We would catch them and tie a string around one leg. Then, holding on to the other end of the string, we'd let them go and watch as they buzzed round and round our heads like little remote control airplanes. And who hasn't caught fireflies and locked them in a jar? I suppose it's just the order of things. Curious boys will take undo advantage of small animals and insects. Again, I'm not saying it's right. I'm just saying they have fun doing it.

Ode to an Apple Tree
(Warning: May be Sentimental)

The food was all free
From that old apple tree
That grew by our home on the hill.
Where the apples were sweet,
The best you could eat.
In my memory I'm tasting them still.

On that old apple tree
I would skin-up my knee
As I climbed for the treasures on high,
Then out on a limb
I would carefully "shim"
And eat my fill in the sky.

It was there on that tree
I came plainly to see
How God feeds the birds and the bees.
With red orbs He hung there
That I plucked from mid-air
He was able to feed even me.

The Big League Pitch
(Summer 1962)

"That's it, Son. Pitch it right in here."

I wound up in a herky-jerky motion and delivered the ball with a sidearm sling.

"Nope, nope. You gotta put a little more spin on it. If it don't break down," Uncle Lawrence motioned with his hand, "it ain't no good. Might as well throw it over the fence."

I was visiting for a couple of weeks with Lawrence and Aunt Lucille who still lived in Detroit. They didn't have any children then and wanted to experiment with having a kid around the house. Guess who got volunteered. So, I was back in the big city again. Admittedly, Detroit still held some attractions for me. The Lone Ranger and Tonto were making a live appearance, the Tigers were in town, and down the street a block or two was an A&W root beer stand. You couldn't get A&W draft root beer in Fayette County, West Virginia in those days. Pity. No drink in the world compared to a tall frosty mug of thick, foamy A&W. The effects of that brew, however, wore off in an hour or two. Mountain Fever lingers for years.

Lawrence had taken me on as a "project". He was going to show me how to throw his famous sidearmed sinking curve ball - his diabolically slow sinking curve ball that drove batters wild. He had had some success as a pitcher in the local leagues that abounded back home in the '50s. Nearly every coal camp had its team and some had connections with the professional leagues. Well, Uncle Lawrence had gained some notoriety back then and actually had a chance to pitch professionally. That is, until he injured his arm.

As an established Senior Little League pitcher who had a 1-0 shutout in the regional playoffs, I wasn't sure what he could teach me that I didn't already know. But it wouldn't hurt to humor him. He'd come in from work in the evening and we'd eat dinner. (Funny, Lucille's green beans didn't taste as good as they used to.) I'd behave like a model child. After all, I didn't want them to go through life childless. Lawrence would then get out the gloves and ball and we'd go out into the yard for a lesson.

We'd pitch for awhile as he would try talking me through all the steps. Hold the ball this way, swing your hips that way, sling your arm the other way, tilt your glove that-a way, and don't forget to snap your wrist and roll the ball over your middle finger as you release it. And "follow through". Don't forget to "follow through". Boy, what ever happened to just picking up the ball and throwing it really hard? Inevitably, Lawrence could not resist demonstrating his famous pitch. It was, indeed, an eye-popper. Approaching the plate slow and straight, it was a pitch no hitter could resist, but I could see how, just when the batter would be committed to swing, the ball would drop as if it had rolled off a table. Armed with that pitch, a guy could go to the majors, if only he could throw it more than eight or nine times without pain.

Later in the evening, Lawrence would sit bare-chested and grimacing as Lucille applied the Ben Gay and hot towels to ease the pain in his shoulder. I read the expression in their faces. I saw how the pain in Lawrence's shoulder could not compare to the disappointment in his heart. We never passed ball again after that visit and I never did learn how to throw his diabolical curve ball.

Fairy Dust Snows

I sorely miss the deep snows - the cold, deep, overpowering, comforting snows of my youth. The Detroit City streets of my early youth were full of them. They provided many an opportunity for castle building and snow battles amongst the neighborhood hedges. Although they came deep and often, somehow they did not compare to the mountain snows of my youth. These were snows born of legends, mingled with fairy dust, and delivered by the Mountain King himself.

I would pray for the fairy dust snow to come. I would watch the changing sky in anticipation. Perhaps tonight, perhaps tomorrow, the clouds would work their magic. Hours before a big storm, the air would tease your nostrils with the hint of snow. The clouds would take on that "just so" gray look and the wind would blow (or not blow) in that "just so" way that would herald the oncoming storm. And then it would come, slowly at first, silently filling the night sky, building in intensity as it covered the ground and trees, and road, and mountains, driving everything into oblivion. I was but a helpless observer as the snow covered everything with its icy mantel, obliterating the world. We mortals were powerless against the snow as it mounted, cutting off pathways, driveways, and roads. We were inextricably drawn into the belly of the storm and the universe was soon reduced to a window and a frozen, isolated valley.

Wrapped safely in my blanket, I would view the snow from my window. That's all there was left of the world. No roads, no cities, no oceans - just me and the storm were all that was left of creation. It was then, when I succumbed to the omnipotence of the storm, that the fairy dust began to work. It would strip me of my cares and fears and bath me, for one brief night, in a snow sea of serenity. My life, my very being, was engulfed in the magic and comfort of the moment. I wished it could last forever. Oh indeed, how I miss the snow storms of my youth, especially the ones salted with fairy dust.

Five foot Eight, One-o-Five

Five foot eight, one-o-five
That's all Mom ever weighed,
But she's never dieted in her life,
That's just the way she's made.
Five foot eight, one-o-five
That's all she ever weighed.
And she's never been in the sun
'Cause I've never seen her make shade.
The only time she ever got "fat"
Was the time when she got the mumps,
But then it was only in her cheeks
Where you could ever see any lumps.

Don't Eat the Green Beans

Now, I never ate Mom's green beans
'Cause she never learned how to cook.
And unless Granny fixed me a mess,
Mom's burnt green beans I forsook.
She did alright with burgers and fries,
Or hot dogs, or potluck stew,
But I wouldn't eat her blackened old beans
And I bet neither would you.

Post Script

You never know how deceitful your family can be. Somehow, while living in Detroit, I got it into my head that Mom could not cook green beans. In those days my Aunt Lucille and Uncle Lawrence were living on the second floor of our house. So, whenever we had green beans I'd ask,"Mom, did you cook these green beans?"
"No, Johnny, Lucille fixed them," came the reply. Lucille would nod in agreement. Assured I wasn't going to die, I'd load up my plate. Lucille fixed the best green beans I've ever tasted. The best, that is, until I tasted Granny's.

When we moved to West Virginia the tradition continued.
"Mom, who cooked this?"
"Granny did."
"Is that right, Granny?"
"Sure is, Little Johnny. Granny cooked 'em 'specially for you."
"OK" - Chow down!"
But you never know how deceitful your family can be. I discovered years later, after both Granny and Lucille had died, that they and Mom had been lying to me big time. Mom had been cooking those stupid green beans all the time. Yep, you never know how deceitful kin folks can be. Now that I've been thinking about it, those green beans didn't taste so good after all.

SupurrrLube

I don't remember Dad ever owning a new car until sometime after I left home and got married. So, he was always tinkering, either out of fun or necessity, with old cars and he was eternally in search of that magic elixir that would revive an old engine for just a few more miles. So, Dad, this poem's for you. (The rest of you folks can read it, too, if you want.)

This SupurrrLube is really good stuff;
You just pour it like oil in your car.
It makes the engine purrrrr like new
But I wouldn't drive very far.
The gunk and the grime, the sludge
And the dirt, it washes right away.
But what they don't tell you at $2.99,
You gotta use a whole can every day.
Miracle oil! Wonders it works.
But I'll tell you straight friend to friend,
The only time you should use SupurrrLube
Is the day you trade your car in.

The Old Rocking Chair
(Warning: Sentimental)

A shorter version of this poem was originally written over twenty years ago shortly after my first daughter was born. I recently revised it into a this poem. This was my first published poem. So, Maggie, this one's for you. Thanks for the inspiration.

With sleep on your fingers and a tear in your eye,
I'll rock you to heaven, so baby don't cry.
And while you are sleepin', a-wanderin' we'll go,
To the rocking chair dreamland that only we know.
Sweet sleep on my shoulder, sweet sleep in my arms
Sweet sleep I'll protect you from all the world's harms.
So, rock to my heart beat and with my soul sway
Till we rock through the darkness to find a new day.

I've sat on the porch swing in heavy dew night
To listen to crickets and wildcats scream fright.
I've picked the wild berries for fresh cobbler pie
And caught me a rattler and spit in his eye.
Heard valley train whistling call from afar
And lain in night grass amid shooting star.
I've seen the big cities; I've flown in the air,
But nothing beats my baby and that old rocking chair.

That old rocking chair gives me far more bliss
When I hug up to you and give you a kiss.
Just rocker and me and my sweet baby girl
Wrapped up in my arms and loved for the world.

Ode to Country Music
(Warning: Corn Country)

I'm sure you've heard of backward masking, you know, messages on a song that can only be heard when it is played backward. Well, there is an old joke that goes like this:
Q: What do you get when you play a country song backward?
A: You get your wife back, you job back, your freedom back, your health back....

Now, I really like some country music but some of it is really depressing: lost love, lost friends, lost dogs, etc. And so, to counter balance the tragic stuff, I've written this upbeat *Ode to Country Music* which, I think, touches the very heart of this music genre. Since this is an ode, pick out a country tune (almost any one will do) and try singing along (provided you're alone right now).

Baby parted my hair with a bottle
The other night at the bar.
So, I straightened her teeth with a tire iron
That I pulled from the back of the car.
The blood and the spit, they were flying
As I straighten those teeth that were gaped,
But my dentistry work was stopped short
When the handcuffs on me were slapped.
Now I heard her say
As they drug me away
And my freedom from me to rob,
"Three thousand bucks I paid for these teeth
But you did a much better job!"

(Chorus)
Now, Baby's got the prettiest teeth
That you'll ever find in these hills,
But I'm pining away in this old prison cell
Paying my dentistry bills.

(Deep breath - there's more ....)

(Second verse)
Now, my Pappy's words I'm recalling
As the liquor clears from my head.
Those sweet precious words that he taught me
On the day just before he dropped dead.
He said, "Son, you can kick your old hound dog.
You can even cheat on your wife.
But go fixing folks teeth in a barroom
And you'll be locked up the rest of your life."

Now the train's pulled away,
I'm locked up to stay,
Gramma lives in a truck on the street,
And my wife and kids will go hungry tonight,
But man, Baby's teeth sure look neat

(Chorus)
Now, Baby's got the prettiest teeth
You'll ever find in these hills,
But I'm pining away in this old prison cell
Paying my dentistry bills.

Post Script

Since we're in a silly mood here's one more.

You're not as pretty as you used to be
But you're not as ugly as my wife.
You're not as young as you used to be
And you won't be for the rest of your life.

Or this one ...

I said, "Your Honor, I ain't no fake.
I always keep promises I make.
We'd said to each other, 'Til death do us part'.
That's why I drove a knife through his heart."

Musical Memories

Indulge me a little, please. This section was written purely for my benefit and may mean absolutely nothing to you. However, at the end I'll tell you how you can rewrite this section for your own personal use. You might say you can help write this book or begin writing one of your own. So, bear with me, you'll get your turn in a minute.

Here for my own private consumption is a list of the top ten tunes of all time (pre-1966). They were selected, not for their musical merit, but for the memories they invoke. Some may even be a bit obscure, but that's OK. After all, this is my own private list.

1. *Johnny Angel / Soldier Boy*

    Kissing Alice Whatshername after the school carnival in the eighth grade. This whirlwind romance lasted one weekend, maybe two, but the magic of young romance lingers on.

2. *She Loves You / I Want to Hold Your Hand* (Beatles)

    Playing basketball in the school gym on Saturday mornings. Playing the pinball machine and eating footlong 'dog meat' hot dogs at Tom's Carry Out. Tom's still in business, I think.

3. *Sixteen Tons* (Tennessee Ernie Ford)

    Spending the summers at Granny's, eating fresh cucumbers, fishing, collecting scrap iron, telling Granny that I was going to buy her a tractor for her garden when I made my first million.

4. *The Man Who Never Returned* (Kingston Trio)

    You remember the story of a man named Charlie who got on the Mass Transit in Boston and couldn't get off because he had lost his only dime for the fare. The chorus goes *"He'll never return / No, he'll never return / and his fate is*

still unlearned (What a pity)/ He will ride forever in the streets of Boston/ He's the man who never returned..."
Memories of summers in Detroit, my Uncle Lawrence A&W root beer, and playing baseball in the alley.

5. *(I Can't Get No) Satisfaction* (Rolling Stones)

Spending the summer at a National Science Foundation Camp at Centre College in Danville, Kentucky, seeing the Cincinnati Reds play baseball in old Crosley Field, visiting the horse farms, kissing Susan Whatshername (no relation to Alice) while sitting in a deserted football stadium at night, eating French fried onion rings, seeing outdoor plays and learning to dance.

6. *Louie, Louie* (Kingsmen)

Playing "Post Office" at birthday parties. For those of you who don't know how to play, here's the rules. A room (or closet) was designated as the "post office". Someone was selected to go into the post office who would then call a person of the opposite sex (I'm not sure that restriction would apply today.) of their choice into the room. They would exchange a kiss, the first person would return to the main party room, and the person left in the post office would call someone else. It was a great way to catch a cold and find out who the best and most popular kissers were.

7. *Duke of Earl*

Riding in Wilkie's purple roadster through the New River Gorge on the way to a basketball game. Today there's a multi-million dollar bridge that spans the gorge some 700 or 800 feet above the river below. In those days, however, you wound your way down a one-and-a-half lane road, crossed the river on a rickety bridge and wound your way back up the other side of the gorge through hairpin turns. It was much more of an adventure then, especially riding in Wilkie's purple roadster.

8. *Wild Thing*

You remember, "*Wild Thing, you make my heart sing...*" Sneaking guys into the drive-in movie in the trunk of your car only to discover that it's Family Night and you could have brought a whole car load of people for the price of one. Then getting kicked out for sneaking people in. Bummer.

9. *Mashed Potatoes / Return to Sender / Monster Mash*

Roller skating with Linda Whatshername (no relation to Susan or Alice).

10. *Bingo*

Who knows this one? "*I had a dog down on the farm and Bingo was his name / B-I-N-G-O, B-I-N-G-O, B-I-N-G-O / and Bingo was his name.*" Memories of kissing Ann Logan in the back seat of a car on the way to a church youth rally. At last I finally remembered a last name! Bingo!

OK, I told you the list was for my personal consumption. Now its your turn. Get a pencil and piece of paper. (I don't want you marking up my list.) Now go make your own list. Dig deep, go back as far as you can, and make it personal. Scan your memory banks and, perhaps, pull out some memories that will surprise yourself. Now try and put dates on the events. Was it summer or winter? Was that 1961 or 1957? What was that person's last name? Now go write yourself a book, after you've finished with this one, of course.

The Night Visitor
1962

We eagerly welcomed the new night visitor. For a time, it drew our attention away from the normal sights and sounds of the night. It competed well with the lighting bugs and stars. Our new night visitor was named Telstar. It was a space communications satellite and everyone was excited about it. Telstar and its successor Telstar II paved the way for transatlantic and, eventually, worldwide television transmissions. Folks today don't get too excited about satellites. In fact, we rarely see them or give them a thought and, yet, all of our worldwide communications are dependent upon these tiny machines out in space. Apathy, however, was not the case in 1962. You must recall the times.

World War II and the Korean conflict were fresh in the country's mind. The Communist threat was ever present, and we were in a make or break space race with the Soviets. One small inkling of the mood in those days could be seen in the one difference I found between Detroit and West Virginia schools. We didn't have air raid drills in West Virginia, but we did in Detroit. Just like a fire drill, the bell would ring, and we would all line up and proceed to the school's basement to sit with knees tucked under our chins until the drill was over. That all seems a little strange to me now, but it was serious business back then. (I do recall one other difference in the schools. The only time I every had to walk to school was in the city. These stories you hear of walking barefoot to school through ten miles of mountains in a foot of snow in April are fairy tales. We had buses in those mountains that dropped us off right at the front door.)

Telstar was launched in the summer of 1962 and served as a very present symbol of America's progress in the space race. The exciting aspect of Telstar was that it was visible with the naked eye. Schedules were printed in the paper and people across the nation flocked to the night sky to watch it orbit every few hours. The folks on Loop Creek were no exception. The whole community (if you can call six houses and a gas station a community) gathered in our neighbor's yard and awaited its arrival. Bobbie Kay would snuggle up close to me as the night chill fell upon us. Then, right on time, a small speck of light would rise above the high peaked mountains in the west, silently streak across the sky, and disappear into the trees of the eastern horizon.

We gazed silently at the man-made wonder in the sky and began to contemplate what this marvelous new technology would bring. Would we travel to the moon? Would people be living in space stations someday? Would space travel be as common as airplane flights? America was entering into a new era of technology which would challenge and bend our moral fiber by the pace of its development. A short year and a half later President Kennedy would be shot dead on the streets of Dallas, driving a stiletto into the very heart of this nation, and launching us, unwillingly, upon a national soul searching odyssey. Thirty years later, we're still trying to cope with this new technology and we still haven't reclaimed and repaired our nation's soul.

The Garden

Tired, worn, ripe,
Pregnant,
The garden yields treasures
In autumn crisp glow.

Turnips, corn, pumpkin
Baking potatoes
Siphoned from earth and sky
Sprung from the ground
Burdening buckets
Overloading the truck
Filling the crib.

Harvest is over
Winter's to come
Spent, exhausted
The garden lies quietly
Awaiting winter's sleep...
Work is done.

Post Script

  Dad had two friends named Todd and Wilbur. In my mind, they were a matched set. I never thought of them as Todd and Wilbur, but rather as Todd-n-Wilbur. Financially, Todd-n-Wilbur were in the plumbing business, but they were in the farming business spiritually. And Dad had joined forces with them.
  Together they were working a bottom beside the creek about three miles from Granny's house. (For you Ohio-type folks, the phrase "bottom beside the creek" is redundant. The only place you'll ever find a bottom is beside a creek.) Dad would do all the repairs on the tractor and rig special equipment with his welder. Todd-n-Wilbur would do all the plowing and planting. But we all shared in the harvest.
  The activity at harvest could almost be depicted by a series of country clichés. Scene I: Dad and I are riding in the back of

an old truck as Todd-n-Wilbur drive down a dirt road. Scene II: the truck stops beside a small white country farm house and Todd-n-Wilbur get out of the truck in their bibbed overalls. (Thank goodness, Dad didn't wear bibbed overalls.) Scene III: We walk a swinging bridge across a tranquil tree-lined creek to the garden. Did I actually live this or is this a Norman Rockwell flashback?

The garden didn't look very promising at this time of year. The weeds and thistles had overtaken the "good" plants. If I parted the weeds, I could find the remains of a potato plant or two. Occasionally, I would see the purple tops of turnips which had been randomly sown in late summer. As I stood in the weak, warm, autumn sun, I could see that even the weeds, betrayed by their own biological clock, were beginning to die and turn brown. No, the garden at this time of year did not look promising.

But beneath this apparently worthless growth, lay the treasure. As Todd-n-Wilbur plowed the furrows, potatoes sprung from the earth. Dad and I loaded them into baskets and then into a cart that would later be pulled across the creek to the truck.

I knew then, in the harvest, why Todd-n-Wilbur and Dad were into farming. There is, indeed, something spiritually satisfying about digging your own crop out of your own land - especially when you realize that it ain't really your land and it ain't really your crop. It is, rather, the fruits of the labor of the garden itself whose caretaker, in the final analysis, is God. In a very real sense, we were , and are, just heirs to the fruits of their labor.

I have yet to sense that transcendence preparing a microwave entree. Probably never will.

There's a Bear There Somewhere!
(Pure fun just for kids)

There's a bear there somewhere!
In all of those trees,
But I can't see him
For all of those leaves.
There's a bear there somewhere!
In all of these woods,
But I can't see him
Like I think I shoulds.
There's a bear there somewhere!
I wish I could see
That big bear somewhere
Who's looking at me.
Just wiggle your ears,
Or stick out your nose,
Or show me the claws
On the end of your toes.
There's a bear there somewhere
Who won't show his face
Though I've looked and looked
All over this place.
I know he's there somewhere,
I'll just have to believe
There's a bear there somewhere
That I cannot see.

Faith is the beauty of life. Be beautiful.

Tall Tales and Other True Stories

"I am always at a loss to know how much to believe of my own stories."
                                        Washington Irving

"In winter's tedious nights sit by the fire with good old folks, and let them tell thee tales ..."
                                        Shakespeare

"Once upon a time ...."   Gramma Goldie

"Truth is better than fiction, except when fiction makes a better story."

                                        John Kincaid
                                        City Boy, Country Heart

The Butcher and the Hound Dog
1964

Watch out for your neck when you're thumbing.
That's what all my friends said.
'Cause the next time you stick out your thumb
You may just ride 'til you're dead....

A body neatly cut into pieces
In a duffle bag, so we were told,
Was found atop Gauley Mountain
Lying there beside of the road.
In the hills of the New River Valley
A mad butcher was loose on the run
And we all were shocked and astonished
By the ghastly deed he had done.
When Beggar Jim disappeared from his alley
And the victims started to mount,
You were carefully watching behind you
When 'e'er you were out and about.

Then late one night from a ball game
With my car all broken down,
(My friends had left just a minute ago)
I needed a ride home from town.
At sixteen (and a half) there are some things you do
That on hindsight really look dumb.
Like driving at night without any lights
Or riding back home on your thumb.
Well, I thumbed down a ride; hopped inside.
Then I knew it wasn't my day
When the driver said as we sped through the dark,
"I can only take you part way".

I got out when he turned at the junction
And in darkness stood all alone.
With the night black as sin and fog settin' in
I felt the fear in my bones.
When a hound dog growled in the darkness,

I knew then my prospects were thin,
But a truck topped the hill; stopped by my thumb.
The driver said, "Hi, son, get in."
He wore a hat and spoke with a grin.
Did I detect a slight sense of swagger?
The dome light came on as I opened the door.
There in the seat lay a dagger.
He saw what I saw, so he picked it up,
Threw it back with the rest of his gear.
He said, "Son, don't go worryin' 'bout that."
"I use it for skinnin' my deer." (,my dear?)

The hound dog growled close beside me
And I knew I was in quite a stew.
"Come on, boy, get in! I can't wait all night."
"I got me some skinnin' to do."
I looked long and hard at that truck.
There was no deer in its bed.
Now, a hound dog's teeth may skin you alive,
But it beats being skinned when your dead.
So I slammed the door quick in his face
And lit out down the road in a flash.
Now, me and that hound dog hold the world's record
For doing the twenty mile dash.

Post Script

In the mid-1960's a series of gruesome murders occurred in the area. The murders remain unsolved to this day. The victims were hitchhikers and street people whom the madman would butcher like hogs. Was my encounter with the Mad Butcher fact or fiction? Only he knows for sure.

The Boy Who Never Struck Out

Star of the team,
Batted fourth.
Pitched as oft' as I could.
Bases loaded,
Stepped to the plate.
The pitcher shook where he stood.
Confident swing,
Sky high drive,
The fielder stumbles to fall
Into the fence,
Covers his head,
And his glove is caught by the ball.
Next time up
Bases are full.
There'll be no denying this blast.
Lofty and long
From bat goes the ball.
I've got my grand slam at last.
Rookie in right,
Back peddles hard,
Cap flies away near the wall,
Tumbles down,
Looks all around,
And there in his glove lies the ball.
Last chance today,
They're loaded again,
I'll blast that ball with my might.
Pity-pitched ball,
Hangs in mid-air,
As I violently knock it to flight.
Big universe.
Questions galore.
There's things I don't understand,
Like rounding first
And seeing the fielder
Wave my home run in his hand.

My apologies to *Casey at the Bat*.

Kamikaze Midnight
1963

We once had a black Mexican Chihuahua appropriately named Midnight. He had a companion named Boy. Boy got his name because no one could agree on a name. In the meantime my sister Karen kept calling to him "Here boy. Here boy" when she fed him. Soon the only name he'd respond to was "Boy".

Boy was a brown, beagle-type mutt to whom Midnight looked for guidance and moral support. You see, Midnight was really a half-breed. He was half dog and half chicken and, so, he never did anything without Boy's leadership. If Boy barked, Midnight barked. If Boy chased a car, Midnight chased a car. If Boy retreated, Midnight retreated even faster. He was sort of a dog's version of Barney Fife.

Well, one day something got into that dog and he did something totally out of character. The two had taken to a bad habit of chasing cars as they pulled from the nearby gas station. Of course, Boy would lead the way. Well, this day Midnight acted on his own; Boy was nowhere in sight. As a car pulled from the station, Midnight raced barking from the porch, barreled down through the yard, and in an act of misjudgment "kamikazed" into the front hubcap of the car.

The driver probably never felt the impact; the dog was so small. But the impact left poor Midnight lying there beside the road on his back with his legs pointed straight and still into the heavens. I ran to the road and my uncle Jeep, who was mowing the grass at the time, came running with me.

"Is he dead?" I asked fearing the worst.

"Don't, know," said Jeep, "Might-a broke his neck."

We looked down to inspect him. He appeared to be uncut. There was no blood, not even from his mouth. But there he lay motionless with his feet straight up in the air. Just then, the little body gave a quiver. There was hope.

"Perhaps, he's just knocked out," I said, expressing the hope I'd just saw.

"Yeah, maybe," Jeep said, not quite so optimistically. "Let's try this."

He went back to the lawn mower and dipped some gasoline on a rag.

"Poor man's smelling salts," he explained as he waved the rag under the dog's nose.

At first nothing changed. The dog remained motionless. But as Jeep passed the rag under its nose again, something began to happen. Midnight began to quiver more and more until, at last, he as shaking violently. Suddenly, he arose from his stupor and ran around in the yard, yelping and shaking his head wildly in pain. And then, just as suddenly, he keeled over in the grass. I ran to his side and looked down. He was motionless again, his feet again in the air.

"Is he dead, Uncle Jeep?," I asked as tears rose uncontrollably in my eyes.

"Nope, Just outta gas," he replied as he waved the rag under the dog's nose once again.

Post Script

Every word of this story is (almost) true. Midnight did live to chase more cars and this encounter seemed to make him bolder. Once he had cars stopped in both directions as he darted back and forth in each lane. Boy wasn't quite that crazy.

Josiah Came Knockin'
1964

Early one morning 'bout half past four
Josiah came knockin' home on his door.
It was the deadest of knocks in the deadest of night.
He woke the whole family; Mom turned on the light.
Who could that be so soon in the morn
Who comes knockin' this way so long before dawn?
"Who is it?" they called. "It's Josiah, your son."
Pop pulled on his pants; Annie went with a run.
Mom looked at Pop. "How could this be?
Josiah's miles away in the military.
He won't be home for two months or more.
So how is he knockin' now at our door?"
When to the door Annie pressed hands and ear
She felt apprehension, a slight twinge of fear.
"Is that you, Josiah?"; "Yes, Annie, it's me."
"So open the door and do it quickly!"
But when they opened the door, no one was there,
Just the still of the night with light fog in the air.
"Mom, Pop," Annie said with fear in her soul,
"Josiah was here, but where did he go?"
Later that day, the state trooper came.
He shook Papa's hand, called him by name.
He said, "Jess, I think you'd better go get your wife."
The news that he brought them cut like a knife.
Josiah had gotten a short three day pass.
He'd set out on the road and started home fast,
But his plans and his life would end in a flash
When the car he was riding was involved in a crash.
And the time that it happened? (Now, folks, this may shock.)
Was the same time that morning when they heard him knock.
Yes, early one morning 'bout half past four
Josiah came knockin' home on his door
For one last good-bye to his folks and his kin
'Cause he knew they'd never see him again.

"Annie" told me this story at "Josiah's" wake. You don't make up stories like that at your brother's funeral.

The Mean, Green, Running Machine
1968

It was a mean, green,
Running machine,
Ran a notch or two out of time.
A hundred chipmunks under the hood.
The steering wheel really looked good.
That mean-green machine was all mine....
I had an '60 Renault.
I don't mean to find fault.
It got forty miles to the gallon of water.
And the engine ran fine
Well, some of the time
But it rarely ran like it oughter.
Dad tried time and again
The engine to mend.
Oft times it was out on the table.
But with all of his skill
And all of his will
Somehow he just wasn't able.
I got in it one day
And sputtered away
When Jane and I left to elope.
And the engine ran fine
Well, some of the time
Especially when you'd go down a slope.
We got to Carolina alright
And got hitched the next night
Then started out to return.
But along 'bout Mt. Airy
Things began to get scary
When the engine started to burn.
Then around Fancy Gap
The pistons went snap
And that mean-green machine ran no more.
A small dime I had
So I called my Dad,
"I'm two hundred miles from your door."

"I'm afraid, Dad," I said,
"That the mean-green is dead.
She's cold and there's no sign of life.
So, will you come today,
Help me haul it away,
And bring Mom to meet my new wife?"

It was a mean, green,
Running machine,
Ran a notch of two out of time.
A hundred chipmunks under the hood.
The steering wheel really looked good.
That mean-green machine was all mine.

Post Script

True story. That old, green Renault was the first car that I ever owned. It had a cracked engine block and blew a head gasket a time or two, but it was all mine, and it only cost a hundred bucks. My wife and I did elope in that old car and drove it down to Cheraw, South Carolina to get married. But on the way back near Fancy Gap, Virginia, just south of the Blue Ridge Parkway, the mean-green passed away. Dad and Mom rented a hitch and came to pull us home. Our luck, however, didn't get any better. Dad's car also broke down on the West Virginia Turnpike as he was pulling the mean-green home. (Yes, my parents and I are still on speaking terms.)

Later, Dad took revenge on the mean-green. He cut the middle out of it, welded the two end pieces together, and made it into a riding lawn mower. Scout's honor.

Laughing in the Face of Death
1978-1989

Only a fool would venture down the New River rapids. At least, that was the local conventional wisdom when I lived in the area. The New, located in southern West Virginia, was (and is) a wild treacherous river. It was beautiful, but dangerous, and sane folks didn't mess around with those New River rapids. And so, I was much surprised when the white-water rafting business began in the early 70's and bloomed into a multi-million dollar industry. So much for that missed business opportunity.

Despite the increasing popularity of white-watering, I managed to stay away from the New until 1978. And then, at age thirty, all sanity must have evaporated from my mortal body. A couple of guys at the office were organizing a trip. They called their great adventure *Laughing in the Face of Death* and invited me to go along. I wasn't too keen on the idea at first, but when everyone in the office started signing up, I knew I was doomed. Besides, I was a local West Virginia boy. How would it look if the transplants from Cleveland went and I didn't? So reluctantly, mostly to save face, I signed up.

After much pomp and planning, the fateful day of the trip arrived. As the guide was going over safety instructions, I became more and more apprehensive. I mean, I grew up near this river. It was great for fishing or looking at. It was even a great place to bring your girl parking after the dance, but you never wanted to get your feet wet. Who knows when some sinister, unseen current would sweep you away into the realm of the catfish. I also started to remind myself just how accident prone I was.

"Remember that scar in your forehead," I said to *Myself*. "Just how did you get that?"

"Trying to open a storm door with my head," *Myself* replied.

"And what about that scar on your ankle?," I queried *Myself* further.

"Just trying to stop a bike by putting my foot in the spokes," *Myself* defended.

"And that two inch hole in your wrist?" I said, pressing my case.

"Oh, that?" *Myself* sighed trying to ignore the facts, "Uh, that's from the handle bars of a bike when I got hit by a car."

"And what about that scar on the top of your head, and the one on your index finger, and that chipped tooth and..." I grilled *Myself*, growing more and more confident of my incompetence.

"OK, OK. So I've done some pretty foolish, unsafe things," *Myself* finally admitted.

"Yea, like white-watering down the New," I said resting my case in triumphal defeat.

By this time, we were in the rafts in the middle of the river and there was no time for panic or retreat. The water battles had begun! People started throwing water from raft to raft with the jugs and buckets brought along for bailing. Everyone caught the battle fever. We were like the great galleys of old: positioning, repositioning, attacking and then falling back or, perhaps, begging for mercy. The water battles really relaxed everyone and, before we knew it, we were into the rapids. The first ones were easy and fun and everyone's confidence grew (including mine). We soon found ourselves anticipating the next rapids, eager to be sweep up in the battle with the river. By the end of the day, after having conquered the untamable river, we swaggered ashore - confident - seasoned - experienced. We had, indeed, *Laughed in the Face of Death* and survived.

This success spurred us on to new highs. Later that year we tackled the Gauley River which is even more dangerous. The next year we redid our *Face of Death* trip. However, my propensity for accidents finally caught up with me. It happened, not on the New, but on a dinky stream called Raccoon Creek. Normally, this is an innocuous little creek for canoeing that can easily be waded across. However, this time, it was a good ten feet above normal due to recent heavy rains. This did not deter us as we launched our canoes into the now Roaring Raccoon Creek. It was a hot day and we had foolishly (funny how that word keeps popping up) taken off our life jackets. Unexpectedly, my canoe was struck broadside by a submerged tree limb and we were capsized. As I came to the surface treading water, fighting the current, groping for the bottom, and dodging tree limbs, one thought shot through my mind: *Fools die like this*. Fortunately, we made it to the bank and, after some struggle, were able to right the canoe and finish the trip.

Although Raccoon Creek gave me a warning, I was not dissuaded from my white-watering ways and returned for another trek down the New. That's when the next "shot across the bow", so to speak, came. One section, known as the swimmer's rapids, allows you to get out of the raft and float through the rapids (in your life jacket, of course). So I jumped out, pointed my feet downstream, and went with the flow. About half way through, I bobbed under the water and emerged with this large black thing on my head. It was the raft. I was under the raft! My mind raced - shades of Raccoon Creek - only fools do the New! This wasn't *Laughing in the Face of Death*. This was *Death Laughing in Your Face*! But again, fortunately, I was able extricate my foolish self from the trap and climbed, humiliated and half drowned, back into the raft.

A little later, I was back in the water floating down the long, deep section called Fire Creek. I was still a little shaken by my UFO (Uncooperative Floating Object) encounter. Suddenly, a mortal fear gripped my mind. Suppose some hitherto unknown behemoth would rise up from its deep water lair and attack my dangling ankles? After all, I had always heard that most fish like the taste of chicken. I climbed quickly back into the raft.

The final "shot" came when my son was thirteen. I wanted to expose him to the "joys" of New River, so I chose a relatively safe activity. Canoeing trips were offered on a quiet part of the river. They were billed for BEGINNERS with NO EXPERIENCE. This would be a piece of cake. After all, I had done the Gauley and the New three or four times. Certainly, I could master this.

I felt smug and superior as the guides taught us how to paddle while standing on the river bank. We entered the water and practiced our paddling for awhile before heading downstream. No water battles - no rowdiness - no rapids - almost. Downstream about a half mile was a small set of rapids. It was nothing by New River standards, but nothing to ignore in a canoe. We were instructed to stay near the left bank in the shallows. Foolishly (there's that word again), my son and I got too far to the right. The current caught us, turned us broadside, and dumped us into the main channel.

We struggled with the canoe against the current and finally managed to drag it up onto a rock in the middle of the river. I looked down at my right index finger which was throbbing wildly. It was split lengthwise from top to bottom, exposing the bone. My son looked at it and laughed. Honest, he actually laughed.

The rest of the day was spent at the hospital getting x-rays and nineteen stitches to close the wound. My son had to shift gears for me on the drive home. Worse yet, two days later we left for vacation at the beach. While the rest of the family was on the beach, I was at the local hospital getting blood tests, antibiotic shots, and bandages changed. But worst of all, my family teased me unmercifully because I had to hold my finger up in the air to keep the swelling down. Everyone in Myrtle Beach new what a klutz I was. You can be assured that the next time I *Laugh in the Face of Death*, it will be on the golf course.

Don't Go Campin' Up Camp Branch Hollow
1960

Don't go Campin' up Camp Branch Hollow.
If you do, you may never return.
My Dad and uncles were serious about this.
It's a lesson they said I must learn.
When they were young, full of spunk just like me,
(Somehow that's hard to believe.)
They went camping one night in the bowels of Camp Branch,
Thus begins the tale they would weave....

'Twas the midst of fall
When witches come call
The boys set their camp in the glen.
'Twas the time of the year
When spirits you'd hear,
But they were the bravest of men.
Round the campfire they sat
And occasionally spat
The tobacco they weren't s'pose to chew,
When straight up one sat,
Whispered, "Man, what was that?"
The others: "I thought it was you."
Then the trees got real still,
From the top of the hill
They heard the faintest of sound.
"It's just an old deer
That all of us hear
A-pawing around on the ground.
Or it might be a dog
Or a squirrel on a log,"
Harry said as he sat on his knees.
Someone told a joke,
The silence it broke,
And the laughter fled through the trees.
Then on their ears fell
The shrillest of wail
And the leaves whipped around in the breeze.
And the Forest moved in

And these bravest of men
Began to get weak in the knees.
Then the mountains went hush.
Their hearts started to rush.
They nearly beat out their throats
When there in the sky
To each panicking eye
A spirit above them did float.
It came white in the night,
A most terrible sight
With hoofs flailing wild in the air.
From its nostrils blew smoke
As the tent poles it broke.
Its red eye had a demonic glare.
Its white tail was long.
Its haunches were strong.
Its teeth were rapier sharp.
The campfire went out
And it let out a shout
As it ripped its teeth through their tarp.
As it reared up its head
Harry cried, "We're all dead!"
As they bolted as one in a spill.
But hot in their tracks
It pressed on the attack,
As this ghoul moved in for the kill.
They fled from the scene
And down the ravine
And out of the hollow they ran,
But when they looked around
No demon they found,
Just the wisp of a white little band
Winding back through the trees
That were shedding their leaves
As the spirit passed by their way.
Then it (poof!) disappeared.
But its presence they feared.
They've never returned to this day....

Now you might think they were trying
To tell a tall tale and deceive

A young boy like me into buying
Their yarn about ghosts to believe.
Their tall tales me believe? Not a chance!
But, now, just between me and you,
I've seen that wisp of light over Camp Branch,
So I know what they're tellin' is true.

Room at the Inn
1975

My wife and I had planned a weekend retreat with another couple. Our friends had arranged to borrow a cabin from one of their friends. The cabin was nestled in the remote Greenbrier Valley of West Virginia and we were planning to relax away from the kids and do some sightseeing.

Someone's schedule must have gotten mixed up because when we arrived at the cabin it was already occupied. As we began searching for another place to stay for the night, we remembered passing a little "Mom and Pop" motel a few miles back and decided that in this neck of the woods that was our only hope.

Pulling up to the office, the four of us went in to register. Since we were planning on playing cards most of the night, we decided to save some money and rent only one room.

"Do you have a room for the four of us?" I asked.

"One room for the four of ya?" the clerk asked, confirming my request.

"Yes, we only need one room," I replied.

The clerk, obviously a seasoned motel operator by anyone's standards, asked without hesitation, "One bed or two?"

Philosophy and Potpourri

"There is nothing so absurd but some philosopher has said it."
Cicero

"'I am ruminating,' said Mr. Pickwick, 'on the strange mutability of human affairs.'
'Ah, I see -.... Philosopher, sir?'
'An observer of human nature, sir,' said Mr. Pickwick."

Charles Dickens
Pickwick Papers

"Philosophy has nothing to do with living, but everything to do with life."

John Kincaid
City Boy, Country Heart

Kimberly

This poem is about my youngest daughter, Kimberly. Kim was born with a congenital hearing loss. She, her mother, and I have struggled long and hard to keep her life as normal as possible. So, this poem is dedicated to the one who taught me *hupomone* (Greek word meaning endurance, patience, victorious perseverance).

Sometimes in anger I've asked You,
But often with most bitter tear,
If You made the earth and the heavens
Then why can my daughter not hear?
I don't want her labeled as "special" -
An excuse to push her aside.
I want folks to look past her frailty
To see the blossoming beauty inside.
But I've seen as she labors in learning,
And heard as she struggles to speak,
And she's taught me with each hard fought victory
'Tis I, and not she, who is weak.
For she's overcome much more in ten years
Than I have in my forty or so,
And she's taught me a life-long lesson:
Sometimes the victories come slow.
So we'll persevere till we've vanquished
Every fear, every failure and foe,
And be better off for the battle
In which she, and I also, will grow.

Lord, thank you for sending her to us
Made in her own unique way.
I'm certain there is a day coming
When I, and she also, will say:
I've played my life's hand to the fullest.
And overcome much more than most.
For my spunk and indomitable spirit
Not I, but in you, Lord, will boast.

The Lie

The lie lay sleeping where I laid it last,
Lying secure within my past,
But lie lay alone not very long
When two more lies were laid along.
Then along lay three and then lay four
To lie there strewn on conscience's floor,
Till lies were laid o'er all my life
To lay on me much pain and strife.
So let this tale sink to your bones:
A lie can never lie alone.
If you eye a lie lying 'round,
Lay lie aside; let truth be found.

   I've always wondered why English has to be made so complicated, especially when it comes to one word that has two different and sometimes opposite meanings. For example, take the word "left" and this sentence: "I was left alone when all of the guests left the party." Here the word "left" means in one sense "to stay" and in another sense "to leave". Another favorite of mine is "ravished". One definition is "to rape violently"; the other definition is "to transport with joy or delight; to enrapture". Come on now, which is it, rape or ecstasy?

Ravished

The lad was ravished; so was the maid.
The next day handcuffs on one were laid.
"I thought you were ravished?"; Came reply: "Most indeed!"
"That's why you will pay for your terrible deed!"

He was ravished; she was ravished.
So reads the court tape,
But when the jury comes in
You'll know who did the rape.

A Poem?

Some folks say a poem's suppose to rhyme
Like "Will you be mine, Valentine",
But you can spend all your time
Making words come out to rhyme
And never once a poem make.
So listen close and get this straight:
You can get all your meter right
And never learn to see the light.
A poem's supposed to make you move
And shake your soul, not make you snooze.
It's suppose to grab your gut
Or crack your brain that's in a rut,
To let a new idea dawn,
Not make you nod or make you yawn,
To make you laugh when you count the cost,
Or give you hope when all is lost,
To wake a soul that's been asleep,
To bring you joy although you weep.
You got to take some common Joe
And make him out some big hero
Or like what's his name - Richard Corey?
You gotta tell a tragic story.
It may be cute, but that's not enough.
You must fill it with profound, weighty stuff.
And if it does not all of these,
Then it ain't a poem, if you please.

The Gift

I searched high and low
For the perfect gift for Christmas day,
And found Him wrapped in swaddling clothes
Asleep on manger's hay.

Blessings

There can be no greater blessing
Than to be drawn inextricably
By our own humanity
Into contact with that
Which transcends our humanness.
To love and to be loved,
To laugh, to cry,
To share from the heart of our soul,
To yearn for peace beyond measure,
To reach out in space and time,
To touch those things,
Which are both infinite and eternal.
Truly these are Gifts of our humanity.
To joy, to sorrow, to despair, to hope,
To dream for what will never be
Until it is.
Truly these are Gifts from God.

Brevity

The old Cook
Shuffled across the room
Ninety-plus years bent in his spine
To recall his life
And heralded ancestors
All in ten seconds time.
Family?
Well, some here and some there,
But they rarely, if ever, show.
Cooks settled these hills -
Out of ninety-plus years
It's the one thing he wants you to know.
Down the hall
Rattling his cane
And silent on sofa he sat.
In all of my life,
I've always believed
Ninety years would take longer than that.

Mountain Math

Don't measure a man by the miles he has trod,
But by how close he's traveled toward the mind of God.

It's not the length of pages,
But the depth of thought that makes a book.

It's not the breadth of knowledge
Nor the depth of thought,
But the depth of communication
That makes a teacher.

You don't have to live on the mountain top
To have a good point of view.

Sometimes the best view of the stars
Is from the floor of the valley.

One of Pappy's old sayings: "Son, you'll never know what true bliss is until you get married - and then it's too late."

My favorite chicken joke: Why did the chicken cross the road?
To prove to the possum that it can be done.

Sticks and stones may break my bones
But names will kill my spirit
And the knife goes deep and the pain shoots high
Every time I hear it.

Conceit

Wrap your arms around me, Babe
And put me under the tree,
When it comes to Christmas gifts
I'm the only one you need.
Put a little bow in my hair,
I don't need nothing else.
Just wrap me up in your arms
And give me to yourself.

That diamond ring in the store
Won't keep you warm at night
But with your arms around me, Babe
Everything's gonna be alright.
So throw away your wishing list,
Forget that shopping spree,
'Cause when it comes to Christmas gifts
I'm the only one you need.

Heyday Hole

What once support miners' loads,
Now's forgotten; known by few.
Ribbons of ruts
Once filled with wheel and hoof, chain and boot,
And barefoot toes,
Now twisting, turning, undulating,
Harmonizing with the croaking creek,
Playing children's tag along the way
To secrets high and deeper than
The heyday hole itself.
Hollow children
Hollowed men
Soup and beans, coal and dust
Livelihood and explosive destiny
Quickly forgotten.

Butterfly Biology
(Just for the kids)

Nothing's more majestic that ever will fly
Than a beautiful Monarch butterfly.
It starts as an egg on the side of a tree,
But when it hatches, a larva it be.
Then it munches on leaves night, morning, and noon,
And when it grows big it spins a cocoon.
All bundled inside the pupa lies "dead".
Weeks later it moves and pokes out its head.
Then suddenly emerges, spreading its wings,
Taking flight through the sky as all the birds sing,
"Raised from the dead to glory the earth,
Fly, butterfly, you're destined from birth
To rise above trees for a short little while
Adorning the summer, enthralling a child."

Cosmic Handcuffs

In youth we wear them proudly
A gift from Mom and Dad
Tiny cosmic handcuffs
Graciously accepted
Thoughtlessly used
Barely noticed shackles
Constant reminders
Of time we do not have

Trophies

Row upon row
Row upon row
Silent warriors
Row upon row
Hands upon knees
Row upon row
In full battle dress
Row upon row
68 Champions
Ten, one and o
Smile at the camera
Row upon row

All State Tackle - 75
Class "A" Champs - 59
Row upon row
Row upon row
Warriors victorious
Row upon row
"Jimmy Tilden's memorial fund
Died in battle, Vietnam"
"This plaque presented
In memory of ..."
"To the greatest coach
With all of our love."

Row upon row
Row upon row
Young men of valor
Row upon row
Carpenter, welder,
Lawyer, drunk,
Teacher, wife beater,
Miner, punk,
Stood once as one
In victory's glow
On autumn green fields
Now covered with snow.

Danger in the Newsprint

Hidden in the morning news box
The cruel trap is laid
Where amid the fact and gossip
A deadly game is played.
From the start it is designed
To be misread with ease
And those tantalizing tidbits
Are contrived but to deceive.
Danger lurks near every corner,
What's woven there's a lie.
To negotiate safe passage
Requires the keenest eye.
Many fools have vainly perished
Checking out the morning news,
When ignoring all the warnings
Into the trap they flew.

What seems so small and harmless
May deftly one's life steal,
While perusing through the headlines
Fools become the morning meal.
But as the paper is retrieved
A higher power intervenes
The deception's swept away
The culprit scrambles from the scene.
Yet this master of deceit escapes
To his paper box retreat
To compose again his twisted theme
And diabolic deeds repeat.

The Siege

Amidst the bird-nested tree
And salamander rock the battle was joined.
One held the mind; the other held time.
One held power; the other held time.
When will the feeble concede to her demands?
Patiently she waits for the slightest foothold
To exploit into a frontal attack.
Keep constant vigil.
Guard the flanks by day, by night,
Shore up the trenches,
Mend every break in the defenses,
Mow down this enemy
Lest the smallest seed of destruction take root.
But finally,
Worn by the multitude of summers,
Broken by the multitude of winters,
Deserted by its maker,
The old mountain road succumbs to the siege,
Rejoining the forest growth.

The Hunter and The Prey

She was slim as fence rail, sweet as a pie
And he vowed he would have her, if not, he would die.
"No love has been deeper, never more true,
 And if robins have feathers, then I will have you."
But she fled like a field mouse,"Oh, no!" she would cry
As she beckoned him onward with a wink of her eye.
And so, he pursued her like a fox chasing hen.
If he could but catch her, her love he would win.
From time immemorial gardens have grown,
Fields have been planted, seeds have been sown,
And boy has chased girl for the wink in her eyes
And long legs like split rails and kisses like pies.
But oft times the hunter ends up the prey
Like the love sick lad on *her* grand wedding day.

PSALM 10111
(THE 23RD PSALM FOR MODERN MAN)

TECHNOLOGY IS MY SHEPHERD: I SHALL NOT WANT.
IT MAKES ME LIE DOWN ON GREEN ASTRO-TURF.
IT LEADETH ME BESIDE CHLORINATED WATERS.
IT RESTORETH MY ENERGY SHORTAGES.
IT LEADETH ME IN THE PATHS
OF THE SCIENTIFIC METHOD FOR ITS NAME'S SAKE.
YEA, THOUGH I DRIVE THROUGH THE VALLEY
OF THE SHADOW OF CHEMICAL WARFARE
I WILL FEAR NO EVIL; FOR THOU ART WITH ME.
THY LASER BEAMS AND GAS MASKS,
THEY COMFORT ME.
THOU PREPAREST AN ARBITRATION SESSION
IN THE PRESENCE OF MY FINANCIAL CONSULTANTS.
THOU ANOINTEST MY HEAD WITH
HEXO-CHLOROPHANE.
MY MISTER COFFEE RUNNETH OVER.
SURELY SAFETY AND ENVIRONMENTAL CONCERNS
SHALL FOLLOW ME ALL THE DAYS OF MY LIFE.
AND I SHALL DWELL
IN AN ALL-ELECTRIC CONDOMINIUM
FOREVER.

Post Script

"10111" is the computer's binary notation for twenty three. I've been in the computer business for almost twenty-five years. I have mixed feelings about our technical advances. On one hand, I like the creature comforts and all the gadgets. On the other hand, I wonder what effects technology is having on our basic human nature. Indeed, I wonder if we are losing touch with the real world and moving into a world where everything is available except the truth. This poem is an attempt to poke some fun at those who rely too heavily on technology for their answers.

The Unbroken Circle

"We shall not cease our exploration
And the end of our exploring
Will be that we arrive where we started
And know the place for the first time"

        T. S. Eliot

It was a soft song
A strong and soft song
A strong and soft song of the hills
Played to the tune of innocent dreams
Young and innocent dreams
Young and innocent plain-folk dreams
Harmonizing our song of the hills.
Spring onion grass
Fresh mowed spring onion grass
Repeats that soft song of the hills.
And it's a strong song
A soft and strong song
A strong song too few of us hear.

        John Kincaid
        City Boy, Country Heart

Universe Central

You may be surprised when I tell you.
This sounds dumb, so don't give me that stare.
Granny's porch swing's the center of the universe.
All roads begin and end there....

You could easily pass by on the highway
And not recognize where you've been.
But when the time lines converge,
Swift ahead in the curve,
Lies that old porch swing again.
Spin your odometers, scramble your clocks,
Rocket to the outermost spaces,
But when you come 'round again,
(As you will, I contend.)
Those porch swings hold prominent places.
It marks the end of beginning; the beginning itself,
Where young as a boy I came out,
Who has become now a man
And can fresh understand
What that porch swing of old was about.
It is universe central, the self-starting place,
The safe where all memories are stored.
Roads lead out, 'round and in,
And back out again.
I know you've been there before.
It may appear to you like a clubhouse,
Or the warmth of that once special room,
Or that view you could see
From your own private tree
That lives still inside youth's cocoon.
There are mysteries at universe central
That cut to the core of us all.
We must stop now and then
To remember us when
Or into the abyss we shall fall.
So come, you and I,
Let us sit on your porch swing
While memories of mysteries play in our heads ....

The High Way Home
1962

That old dirt road was a real mystery to a 14-year-old. I knew where it started, but I didn't know where it ended. You always have to know where things end. I'd been as far as the blackberry patch, but no further. And so, one day I decided to do some exploring.

The road started near Eddie Brown's house just west of and across the creek from Granny's house. It wandered along and waded through a small branch that ran up Camp Branch Hollow. About a mile up it forked. The right fork led to Granny's blackberry patch, a veritable delight in summer. It was the left fork that was unexplored. As I walked along, the road became deeply rutted and clogged with weeds and briers. The road was impassable in a vehicle, but as I persisted the thorns gave way, and I was rewarded by an open road to the top of the mountain and the remains of an old strip mine.

I was walking along the old high wall when, unexpectedly, rounding a bend, the road opened to a view of the valley below. There was the gas station, my house, and Granny's house. I could envision the daily routine going on below. For sure, Eddie Brown was pumping gas or selling my brothers or sister candy and pop. Mom and Granny were either in the garden or preparing dinner. Midnight and Boy were probably lying in wait for a car to chase. There was a certain perverted sense of divinity being up there. You were connected enough to know what was going on, but not close enough to get hogtied into picking beans. I liked the feeling.

As I continued, the road began to descend and I lost sight of the valley. In anticipation, I wondered where this road would end. And then, there it was. I could see my Aunt Jo's house on the hillside below. I'd always wondered where the road that ran past her house led. Now I knew. I was soon back on the main road about two miles east of home.

I walked back down the main road and into Granny's yard, stopping and sitting down on her porch swing to contemplate my adventure. I looked down the road to Eddie Brown's house where the strip mine road "began". Then I turn and looked up the road to the mountain where the strip mine cut a brown band around its top. I had been up there only two hours earlier. In my mind, I could now transport my "divine" self to that lofty spot at any time and look back down upon my mortal self sitting in the swing below. This new-found mental trick gave me a whole new perspective on things. It would be nice to visit the mountain top from time to time, but I could not live up there. That had to be done in the valley. I looked further east and surveyed in my mind how the strip road wound down past my aunt's house and "ended" as it reconnected with the main road.

A sense of accomplishment swept over me. In a very small way, I had proven T. S. Eliot right. There's a deep satisfaction in realizing how things are connected. There's an even deeper peace in knowing your place.

Post Script

Another of my road exploits involved an old county road that ran from Kincaid to Mossy. It was barely passable by car, but I was armed with a bicycle. As I reached the summit of the road, I left my bike and climbed to the mountain top. And there, as I looked over the other side, was the old strip mine road. And there in the distance was Granny's house. That house, I thought, must be the center of the universe. I would return over this mountain several times, partly for the view, but mostly because once you reached the top, you had a four or five mile coast down the other side to the West Virginia Turnpike.

Thirty years later, I would make my last trip over this mountain. This time it was from the Mossy side. With the family in our trusty Suburban, we left the Turnpike at Mossy and started over this little mountain road. We passed a "four wheeler" and the folks turned and looked at us as if we were crazy Ohioians who had lost their way. I soon discovered why. The mountains had done a good job of reclaiming the road. As we drove on, the weeds grew up to the hood and the trees extended down over the windshield. We were in a sea of green. But I was committed to pressing forward; there was no room to turn around. (My family thought I should be committed, but in a vastly different way.) Several hairpin turns were nearly washed out and on several occasions we had to get out and inspect the road before proceeding.

Finally, when we reached the summit, the "jungle" gave way to a rocky road. There was a small graveyard of cars at the summit. Some of them were belly up.

"That's the ones that didn't make it off this mountain," I explained.

"Really?!" my ten-year-old son asked wide-eyed, as he settled, unsettled, back into his seat. Soon we were back on the main road at Kincaid. We stopped at the gas station and there was Eddie Brown, still pumping gas and selling snacks after 30 years. The circuit was once again complete, but it would be a couple of years before I would recognize the connection.

The Mountain King
1962

You'll understand and enjoy this story better if you know the song *In the Hall of the Mountain King* by Edvard Grieg. (Yes, country boys know "cityfied" classical music, but I'm not sure it works in the other direction.) You need to know, at least, the first thirteen notes, so you can sing along when the time comes. So, if you don't know this tune, call your local classical music buff, or visit a real music store and get the sheet music. Reading this story without knowing the song is kind of like cooking beans without fatback. It'll lack that little oomph that makes it better. Normally, I try not make things so esoteric, but in this case, it's unavoidable.

Got you music ready? OK, here goes...

There it was in plain view right outside the car window and across the creek. How could I have not seen it before now? True, it was partially hidden by the cut through which the road passed, but it was visible nonetheless. I chided myself for having missed it all those years. But there it was as plain as day and as big as life (pardon the clichés). The train tracks ran right into it. There, outside the car window, lay an abandoned tunnel, an opportunity for adventure within walking distance from my house. How could I have missed this? It must be explored!

At fourteen I was deep into my exploration phase. Anything and everything was fair game - mountains, creeks, deserted roads, strip mines, abandoned buildings - you name it - I was ready to explore it. I had already followed the eternity of abandoned strip mine roads that lay up Camp Branch Hollow where the mountains were slowing reclaiming their lost ground. And I had conquered the nearly abandoned county road that led over the mountains to Mossy. The uncharted course of Loop Creek was slowing succumbing to my Lewis and Clark endeavors and the old abandoned company store had already yielded its secrets to my investigative zeal. This tunnel would be my next conquest.

My exploring was due in part by my youthful curiosity, but it was also driven by something else. You see, I had felt it. Now, when some folks talk about the mountains being alive, they're not talking metaphorically. And I'm telling you straight out - I had felt it. Sometimes on the crest of a ridge or, perhaps, on a cool, dark, tree-lined passage along a valley floor, I had undeniably felt it. I had felt the Presence of the mountains and I was driven to uncover their secret. For the sake of true knowledge and grand mystery, this tunnel had to be explored and quickly.

The tunnel was about six miles from the house and, so, one hot summer day, I set out on foot toward my goal up the railroad tracks. The tracks themselves offered their own adventures. I had become adept at walking the rails. I could easily go the two miles from my house to the ball field without falling off. This walk would give me an opportunity to sharpen my skills even further. Previously unseen fishing holes, mountain springs spilling their water into the creek, an old abandoned house - these all added to the adventure and made the hike easier until, at last, I was there. The tunnel was in sight.

As I approached, I was confronted by the coolness pouring from the entrance. I looked in. Although the midday sun was on full broil, the rocks inside the tunnel were moist; water dripped down in several places. I began to think about those rocks. How many eons had they lay in the blackness of the mountain before being uncovered by man's feeble attempt to shape his environment? If they could talk, what dark mountain secrets could they tell me? There was something primal in that tunnel waiting for me - something visceral.

Unexpectedly, *The Hall of the Mountain King* began playing slowly in my head. A low haunting tune (Boom-boom-boom-boom-boom-boom-boom) - scary tune (boom-boom-boom) - foreboding tune (boom-boom-boom). As the tune continued to play, increasing in intensity, my mind began to race. I had visions of a secret passageway opening up under my feet. A passage that would lead to the very heart of the mountain and the storehouse of its secrets. *Mountain King* was now barreling through the bass notes in full gear, each note pounding upon my imagination, driving it down to new highs. Ogres, goblins, unspeakable *zoa* (Greek: "animated beings") played on my imagination, lurking in that tunnel, ready to snatch me into their fiendish realm. The secrets of the mountains were open to me, but there would be a price to pay.

The draft blew exceptionally cold over my face. Suddenly, the tunnel entrance was impenetrable, as if a translucent steel door had descended over it. I could not bring myself to step inside. The mountains had once again robbed me of their secret.

As I turned and ran back down the tracks in full retreat, I was certain that I could hear a long, low chuckle coming from the tunnel. The Mountain King still reigned ... Boom-boom-boom-boom-boom-boom-boom....

Eddie Brown
February 24, 1992

When I was growing up in the mountains of West Virginia in the early 60's, I knew a man by the name of Eddie Brown. Eddie worked in the gas station next to my house. He didn't own a car, so he would walk to work. Every morning he'd walk up the road beside the creek past my house to open the "garage" as we called it. And every evening he'd return down the road, across the creek, and over the railroad tracks to home at the mouth of Camp Branch Hollow. Before leaving, he would always put half of the station's money in one pocket and half in the other. I guess he thought if someone robbed him they'd only get half of the money. He seemed to me then a bear of a man as he lumbered past my house in the early morning mist. Invariably, he would pause for a minute or two and turn back toward his house to survey the creek or the mountains before traveling on to the station. Each morning he would greet us as we came to the station to wait for the school bus, and each afternoon he was there to wave to us when we returned.

Eddie was always at the garage; we never saw him anywhere else. He had no wife or kids and lived with his parents. Rumor had it that he never left the creek - except to go to the doctor. From my experience the rumor was true. He never left the garage even to get a haircut; the barber came to him. Many times I have seen him sitting behind the counter, or beside the pot bellied stove while the barber trimmed his hair. If there was one thing constant in life, it was that when you pulled in for gas Eddie Brown would be there to greet you.

I was traveling through my old hometown of Kincaid a couple of years ago. In fact, we had just completed our harrowing trip over the mountain from Mossy. A few things had changed, but Eddie was still manning the gas pumps. The old station was now a hair salon, so Eddie had taken up residence at another station a couple of miles down the road. He still did not own a car and now walked three miles each day down the railroad tracks and back. He was now a man in his late sixties, but he had not changed a bit in those thirty years. He was still the same old Eddie Brown that I knew as a kid. I bought some gas and some candy and pop. He let me behind the counter to pick out the candy - just like he did years ago. I introduced him to my family and we talked for a while before I left down the road to Charleston.

That's the last time I saw Eddie Brown. They buried him yesterday. A month earlier on his way to the station, Eddie was robbed and beaten severely with a crowbar. He managed to make it to the station and open it. You see, the station *had* to be opened for the kids who would be waiting for the school bus. However, he never recovered from the beating. Ironically, Eddie was right all along. The robbers only took the money out of one of his pockets.

If by some small chance you're ever through Kincaid, West Virginia, stop at the gas station for a while, survey the beauty of Eddie's mountains, listen to the tranquillity of his creek, and remember Eddie Brown. I know I will.

Post Script

Some may say that Eddie Brown lived a wasted life, having never left Loop Creek to explore the world. I have my doubts. I have seen enough simple people living good lives that I hesitate to make those judgments. I will tell you, however, a hard rock-bottom truth: You don't have to have a "good time" to live a good life. Eddie may have been unknown to the world, but he was well know and loved by his community. A community that stretches out and back to a lot of 40-year-old "kids" like me.

The End of an Era

   News of Eddie Brown's death had the impact of a time warp on me, connecting and fusing 1992 with 1962. Like the circuitous strip mine road, I was led back thirty years to sit again on Granny's porch swing to contemplate my journey. I was again intimately connected to my childhood, but could now "know the place for the first time". And I realized in that connection that I had grown up, despite the world's imperfections, in a child's paradise. Yes, without exaggeration, it was paradise because I was allowed to be a child and the world was my playground. It was not some artificially generated image on a computer screen. It was not some adventure land with artificial flowers and plastic snakes. My childhood world had real flowers - and snakes - and it offered me more wonder, mystery, and adventure than any game the human mind can devise.
   And so I wept for Eddie Brown and the world in which he lived which will soon be no more. And I wept for my childhood paradise lost - not just for me, but potentially for all of us. And so, I wept for us all because, as a society, we have lost the value for childhood. We are too eager to push our children out of their childhood - too eager to see them grow up, to compete, to get ahead, to get out of house. And so, finally, I wept for our children who are being robbed of their mystery. Will they ever hear a panther scream? Will they ever see a Fairy Dust Snow? Will they ever sense the presence of the Mountain King? Or will King Technology finally roust him from his lair and rob him of his mystic? I pray it never happens.

Our Children
Will they ever feel the Mountain King
Or watch the night from an old porch swing
Or know joy just lying on the ground.
Will they ever know and respect an Eddie Brown.
Will You?

And it's a strong song
    A strong and soft song
        A strong song too few of us hear.

Serenity

There's serenity in these mountains
Huddled, hidden here some place
Lies a valley unchanged, unfettered
By our modern human pace.
Where water shines like crystal,
And the forest fills the air,
And the panther lays a-sleeping
In his secret mountain lair.
Where the shade is cool and grassy
With a breeze upon the trees,
For serenity's in this valley
That no one ever sees.
As a boy I often sought it
As I wandered hills and streams.
Knowing certain I could find it
'Cause I'd seen it in my dreams.
There's serenity in these mountains,
Oh, I've felt it very near
Knowing I could apprehend it
Just across that distant hill,
Just beyond the next horizon,
Or just o'er that rocky ridge,
Or down that cool green river,
And across that swinging bridge.
I've felt it hovering in the haze,
Settling with the snow,
Or descending with the dew drops,
Having lit on faint moon glow.
There are some who say they've seen it,
But I just nod at them and grin
'Cause when they try to lead me
They've forgotten where they've been.
Still its reality holds me captive
Oh, how I yearn for the release
Of serenity in these mountains
Where in pursuit I'll find my peace.